Praise for
THE BOOK OF HOUSEHOLDER KOANS

"In *The Book of Householder Koans* Nakao and Marko wonderfully carry into contemporary life the spirit and color of the Zen koan tradition in all its mystery and brazenness—and, at the same time, provide a wonderfully wise, knowing, and light-hearted look at how we can live this one precious unrepeatable human life in beauty. The koan stories they provide (submitted by many of their students) are pithy, funny, and perfectly apt for the times we live in. What a lively book!" —**Norman Fischer, poet, Zen priest, and author most recently of *The World Could Be Otherwise: Imagination and the Bodhisattva Path***

"I was blown away by the force of *The Book of Householder Koans* as it establishes Western Zen as a new center of enlightenment. Roshis Eve Myonen Marko and Wendy Egyoku Nakao present Zen koans, exquisitely digested from everyday life, that retain the ancient and authentic power to stop you in your tracks while they beckon you onward. Read this book, emerging from two female Zen masters' lifetimes of practice, and enter an intimate world that opens your awareness in relationship, work, and current worldly puzzles." —**Grace Schireson, author of *Wild-Ass Zen, Enlightenment Wherever You Are, Zen Women: Beyond Tea Ladies, Iron Maidens and Macho Maters*, and *Naked in the Zendo: Stories of Uptight Zen***

"In this wonderful collection, Eve Myonen Marko and Wendy Egyoku Nakao write that Zen is about letting go of our fixed opinions. One opinion about Zen, when it came to this country, is that it is for monks and priests who live in monasteries or as hermits. In fact, most Zen students nowadays are householders who have issues that are different from those of our ancestor monks in China. The training for priests cannot be the same as the training for householders. Householders' lives are messy. Roshis Eve and Wendy use the ancient wisdom of Zen to illuminate modern-day practice. Their insight and compassion have provided us with an important collection of koan stories that illustrate how Zen can bring deep insight to all meditators, whether householders, the homeless, women, men, or even ordained priests." —Roshi Gerry Shishin Wick, spiritual director of Great Mountain Zen Center, and author of *The Book of Equanimity: Illuminating Classic Zen Koans*

"The only real Zen is the Zen of our actual lived lives. Zen's koans are stories that take us to where we really live, that show us who we are when we let go of the false stories we've been trapped within. The collections of these true stories, which open our hearts, started in China. And China gave us many that we cherish to this day. Others come from Korea and Vietnam and Japan. And now, in *The Book of Householder Koans*, we are given a selection collected from four Western countries by two preeminent American Zen masters. And this is real Zen. These are the true stories of who we have always been from before the creation of the stars and planets. This is Zen made out of our bones and marrow, our tears and laughter. This amazing book is one of a handful written in this time that will be recalled as classics of our way. If you've never practiced Zen, read this book. If Zen has been your way for forty years, read this book. It opens our way and reminds us of where to find it. *The Book of Householder Koans* is a direct pointing to our heart's longing. True stories." —James Ishmael Ford, author of *Introduction to Zen Koans* and *If You're Lucky, Your Heart Will Break*

"*The Book of Householder Koans* is like a sumptuous feast. The teachings, deep rooted in Zen practice, bring to the table all the ingredients of our life, including heartbreak, fury, and joy. This book shows us that in each moment there is an opportunity to enter a gate to wakefulness, receptivity, and love. Savor each morsel!" —Sensei Koshin Paley Ellison, author of *Wholehearted: Slow Down, Help Out, Wake Up*

"*The Book of Householder Koans* is a remarkable, inspiring, and ground-breaking book that revolutionizes the age-old tradition of Zen koan practice and plunges it right into the heart of our contemporary, 21st-century lives. As Zen teachers, authors Nakao and Marko have been deeply immersed for decades in the practice of life clarifying itself right in the midst of its most knotty challenges and confusions. Along with sixty-six new koans gathered from householders around the world, they offer their profound insight and expertise to help contemporary readers spring open even the most seemingly unresolvable of personal, modern dilemmas. Beautifully written, with a life-affirming wisdom and spirit, this book will come to be a modern classic that helps us to live with a clarity, freedom, and joy beyond what we had imagined possible. Open the cover, take the plunge!" —Peter Levitt, author of *The Complete Cold Mountain: Poems of the Legendary Hermit Hanshan* and *One Hundred Butterflies*, and guiding teacher of Salt Spring Zen Circle in British Columbia

"A wonderful book on koans comparable with koan books from the Song Dynasty China. Wendy and Eve pull no punches in laying out Zen practice in daily life and the challenges we face in leading a full and inclusive life. In fact, they leave no places to escape to. They deal with everything: relationship, work, family, aging, addiction, emotion, and ambiguity, to mention but a few. I don't usually read Zen books, yet this one had me riveted from page one. All they left me, after reading, was to just do it." —Roshi Charles Tenshin Fletcher, abbot of Yokoji Zen Mountain Center, and author of *The Way of Zen*

"I wish I'd been able to read the *Book of Householders Koans* to help integrate practice with my everyday life when I started Zen training. This book is not only for householders, it's also for everyone. Using both the rich stories of ancient Zen masters and current everyday people, the authors explore the human journey: relationships, raising children, work, illness, old age, death, how to ground spiritual practice. This book is a guide for collective awakening, as if one were sitting in a circle with friends with everyone being heard from—sharing their questions, dilemmas, learnings transparently and intimately. And from that sharing, the reader's heart-mind-spirit is expanded through the common threads that unite us all, grounded in the everyday, no matter where we are in our life. The wisdom of these two Zen teachers, Egyoku Roshi and Myonen Roshi, is very accessible, encouraging, and freeing. I highly recommend this book—it's a treasure trove, a true find!" —**Nicolee Jikyo McMahon Roshi, marriage and family therapist**

"This beautiful book is an important resource for Zen in our time. This collection opens our eyes to the koan of our life right now. Easy and fun to read, these householder koans are not just for Zen students, but relatable for all. Maezumi Roshi would encourage his students to study the ancient texts, and then he would say, 'I want you to create the modern Shobogenzo (Treasury of the True Dharma Eye).' Reading the householder koans, I felt that I was encountering a fresh expression of true dharma that maintains the spiritual rigor of old texts. I love these new koans. I love how the layout is reminiscent of traditional koan presentation with verses and comments. And I love how relevant these koans are for our time. The authors are encouraging all of us to create our own householder koans, and I am finding myself seeing koans everywhere. It is a lot of fun and encourages me to see my whole life as spiritual practice. Congratulations to the authors for creating a seminal work. It is a gift for everyone who wants to deepen their appreciation of life." —**Anne Seisen Saunders, abbot, Sweetwater Zen Center, and president, White Plum Asanga**

"Amidst the hustle, bustle, and fragmentation of today's world—taking care of the kids, dealing with disappointments and relationships, facing illness and old age—*The Book of Householder Koans* reminds us that koans are not separate from our life but are, indeed, the *stuff* of living and loving. Filled with real-life situations shared by people around the world, this wonderful book takes koan practice to a new level, encouraging us to open to all aspects of daily life and to embrace its richness. This is a book to be savored." —**Diane Rizzetto, author of *Waking Up to What You Do* and *Deep Hope***

"Thank you, thank you, thank you...! At last, here is a book that highlights the awakenings of everyday people in the midst of heart-rending, courageous challenges. Grab a copy of *The Book of Householder Koans* and you will experience a remarkable shift in Zen literature, one that closes the gap between contemporary practitioners and our ancestors.

What a revolution in Zen training, and yet how intimately these wise authors, Eve Myonen Marko and Wendy Egyoku Nakao, align to Buddha's primary teaching: that Buddha nature resides and manifests within each one of us." —**Anita Feng (Jeong Ji), author of the novel** *Sid*, **and guiding teacher at Blue Heron Zen Community in Seattle, WA**

"*The Book of Householder Koans* is a collection of ordinary wisdom, in the highest sense of that word—'ordinary'—wisdom that does not explain, but with knife-edge words points us in the direction of difficult truths. Using the classical form of a Zen koan, with verse, case, and commentary, Eve Myonen Marko and Wendy Egyoku Nakao draw from their deep understanding across years of practice to reveal that the wisdom of ancient Zen ancestors continues to flourish in our modern lives and homes." —**Hozan Alan Senauke, vice abbot Berkeley Zen Center**

"To take refuge in Buddhism means to simultaneously go forth onto a path of liberation and to return home. This collection of householder koans represents the heart of intimate practice, of discovering that the lotus flower of enlightenment cannot bloom without the nutrients of the muddy world of attachments. Marko and Nakao bring forth the entangled vines of American Buddhism that give new texture to the Buddha Dharma." —**Duncan Ryuken Williams, University of Southern California professor of religion, and author of** *American Sutra*

"*The Book of Householder Koans* is a wonderful book for Zen beginners and even intermediate students. It's sensible, kind, intelligent, and practical, with a wisdom that clarifies the obscure and brings the transcendent down to earth." —**Stephen Mitchell, author of** *Joseph and the Way of Forgiveness*

"Traditional koans speak about Zen monks (and occasionally nuns) waking up in a monastery, far from worldly distractions. These koans are for people living 'in the world,' dealing with a small daughter's out-of-control meltdown in the car, changing an aged mother's diaper, facing a brother's ongoing addiction, feeling overwhelmed by electronic communications, or feeling helpless in the face of systemic poverty and violence.

"This book is a great encouragement to me. The authors and all their anonymous contributors remind me over and over that the point is not to rise above these messy difficulties, but to 'learn to live in the skin of the human being that you are.' Moments of rage, shame, awkwardness, regret, become, in this collection, dharma gates. Don't hold back, just be yourself, step up and do what you can do, take care of what's in front of you, which is the whole world. You can do it! Authors Marko and Nakao—I want to say 'Eve and Wendy'—are my dharma sisters and yours, sharing their wisdom and experience with affection." —**Susan Moon, lay Zen teacher, author of** *This Is Getting Old: Zen Thoughts on Aging,* **and co-author with Florence Caplow of** *The Hidden Lamp,* **a collection of koans about women**

"This book contains a refreshing way to work with koans, using the everyday dilemmas and tragedies that have deep import for people and reframing them as koans. It could ignite a modern and very relevant Western koan tradition.

"The ancient koans often begin with the phrase, 'A monk in all earnestness asked . . .' There are weeks or even years of deep pondering hidden in the phrase 'in all earnestness.' The authors of this book have taken the everyday dilemmas that have deep, deep import for their students and reframed them as koans, helping people move from distress to inquiry, and ultimately to a deeper level of understanding of, and equanimity with their lives." —**Jan Chozen Bays, abbot, Great Vow Monastery, and author of** *Mindful Eating* **and** *A Vow Powered Life*

"'I'm a householder who wants to be a forest dweller,' I moaned to Roshi Bernie Glassman one day when the responsibilities of parenting, work, and caring for the elders in my life all felt too much to bear. 'Just wait for Eve and Wendy's book,' he responded enthusiastically. At last, *The Book of Householder Koans* is here, and I can ease into the reminder that the challenges of my everyday life are not hurdles to overcome...rather, they are the path." —**Rev. Barbara Becker, author of the forthcoming** *Heartwood,* **and dean at One Spirit Interfaith Seminary**

THE BOOK OF HOUSEHOLDER KOANS

WAKING UP IN THE LAND OF ATTACHMENTS

Eve Myonen Marko
Wendy Egyoku Nakao

Monkfish Book Publishing Company
Rhinebeck, New York

Paperback ISBN 978-1-948626-08-8
eBook ISBN 978-1-948626-09-5

Library of Congress Cataloging-in-Publication Data

Names: Marko, Eve Myonen, author. | Nakao, Wendy Egyoku, author.
Title: The book of householder koans : waking up in the land of attachments
 / Eve Myonen Marko, Wendy Egyoku Nakao.
Description: Rhinebeck, New York : Monkfish Book Publishing Company, 2020.
 | Includes bibliographical references.
Identifiers: LCCN 2019039462 (print) | LCCN 2019039463 (ebook) | ISBN
 9781948626088 (paperback) | ISBN 9781948626095 (ebook)
Subjects: LCSH: Koan. | Zen Buddhism.
Classification: LCC BQ5630.K6 M37 2020 (print) | LCC BQ5630.K6 (ebook) |
 DDC 294.3/443--dc23
LC record available at https://lccn.loc.gov/2019039462
LC ebook record available at https://lccn.loc.gov/2019039463

Cover art: Finsbury Parlour, 2015, oil on linen, by Helen Berggruen
Book and cover design by Colin Rolfe

Monkfish Book Publishing Company
22 East Market Street, Suite 304
Rhinebeck, New York 12572
(845) 876-4861
monkfishpublishing.com

To Chan and Zen Ancestors, whose koans first pointed the way,
To Taizan Maezumi, whose face-to-face traversed an ocean,
To Bernie Glassman, who plunged deep and wide,
And to householders who practice intimately in this land of
attachments.

CONTENTS

INTRODUCTION

The Mom gives instructions.
The boy looks at his shoes and dances.
The Mom repeats the instructions.
The boy looks into the air and continues to
*   shuffle his feet.*
The Mom gives instructions for the third time,
*   her voice rising in frustration.*
The boy dances away and says, "Mom, why do
*   you have to be such a bitch?"*

The last word got the Mom's attention like nothing else. Tired and overworked, she might well have lost her temper when her son called her what he did. Instead, the word *bitch* caused her to stop and go silent. Her thoughts and feelings, her anger and frustration all came to a sudden halt. What remained? *Bitch.* So she plunged into *bitch*, her householder koan.

Zen koans arose in the Tang Dynasty in China, in the seventh to tenth centuries, in the shape of spontaneous dialogues between teachers and students, almost all male monks. Later, in the Song Dynasty, they were gathered into written collections and, with great license, put into literary form, with additions of pointers, commentaries, verses, and commentaries on the verses. Koans became literary devices, and koan literature became almost as broad and detailed as jurisprudence.

In fact, they were called koans, or kung-ans in Chinese, meaning "public records," implying a comparison of the Chan teacher with a legal magistrate, with the Chan teacher deciding what is delusion, who is deluded, and how to wake up from delusion. Koans were even referred to much as we now refer to legal precedents or past court decisions. For example, one koan can start with the words, "Regarding the matter of the dharmakaya eating food,"[1] referring to a past koan or teacher-student dialogue in much the same way as a modern legal case refers to precedents like "In the matter of Roe v. Wade" or "In the matter of Citizens United v. FEC."

But that's as far as this comparison goes. When we work with koans, searching for an answer or solution by using our rational mind or usual way of thinking gets us nowhere. Koans demand that we forge into ways of seeing and responding that have nothing to do with analysis, or even reflection, and everything to do with spontaneity, playfulness, imagination, patience, and most important, a radical acceptance of life as it is.

What constitutes a koan? It is commonplace now to describe any difficult situation or edge as a koan. We say that it depends on how you work with it. A challenging situation can be reflected on, analyzed, and written down, and your solutions can be repeated endlessly and become dogmas all their own. In fact, all this happened in Chan and Japanese monasteries after the first compilations of koans were made, with various monasteries adhering to their respective set of answers, memorized and transmitted from teacher to student, generation after generation.

That's not the koan practice pointed to here.

A life situation becomes a koan when it has jolted you out of your usual linear way of thinking, out of the dualistic observer/observed modality that we are so conditioned to use. It becomes koan practice when you no longer think *about* the situation but instead close the gap between the subject and the object, between yourself and what you are facing.

Instead of contemplating the circumstance of your life, you plunge into the very sound, smell, taste, and feel of it, and you stay with that in the face of the temptation to back away into the safer zone of observation and commentary. Stories and feelings will probably swirl in the beginning, as they usually do when we first start to meditate, but eventually, with patience and steadfastness, a different kind of realization dawns, arising from the very marrow of things rather than from the superficial mind.

What are the fundamental ingredients of our life? Change, interdependence, cause and effect, and the fluid nature of everything that we refer to as emptiness. These are not just timeless Buddhist principles; they underlie our very existence as human beings, day by day, hour by hour. We find them everywhere: *My son is addicted to opioids, what do I do? I am an aging, lonely woman, and am afraid of the future.* Approaching such situations as koans demands that we align our subjective life, including all its attachments and wishful thinking, with life as it is, unfolding all the time. A gap is implied here; plunging into this gap, we come into visceral contact with impermanence, karma, no-self, and the interdependence of all life.

Instead of asserting our ideas about what should be, we learn to discern wisely based on what is. "Close the gap between yourself and Yourself," wrote Taizan Maezumi, founder of the Zen

Center of Los Angeles.[2] As you settle into Yourself, your capacity to love and respond to suffering—yours and that of all beings—swells and expands.

There are different systems of koan study, just like there are different systems of Zen training. The same was true in China and Japan. Their systems of practice took hundreds of years to form, starting with the change from wandering mendicants to the establishment of the early monasteries, and from there the development of various rules governing every aspect of monastic life, including the rigorous daily schedule of meditation and work, obeisance to senior students, and seeing the teacher. Koan study usually meant seeing the teacher daily in a face-to-face encounter, on occasion as many as four times a day.

What is our system in the West? Make no mistake, we are developing a system of training here just as they did in China and Japan, and it will take a long time, just as it did then. In fact, we are only at the very beginning of our system's evolution. Nevertheless, some things are becoming clear even now.

The large majority of serious Zen practitioners are householders rather than monastics. That includes most Zen priests as well as teachers (priest and lay), who fulfill their teaching and temple functions even as they have families and hold down other jobs. Their lives are full and rich, their attachments many, their energy often dispersed among different channels of work and relationship. They don't usually live and work alongside other practitioners, and they are lucky to make it to the zendo once a week. What system of training will work here? What koans will they cut their teeth on?

The classic Chan koans came out of the life of a monastery: the work in the kitchen and fields, cleaning the monastery, doing meditation retreats, and face-to-face encounters with teachers. Or else they came out of exchanges between monks or from hermit masters living on the tops of mountains.

The koans presented here are real-life situations submitted by householder practitioners from four different countries. They concern love, raising a family (and especially small children), relationships with friends and neighbors, the rush and bustle of work, connections between men and women, caregiving to those who are old or ill, and preparing for death.

The comments we provide show how to work with each situation as a koan. We discerned each koan's relevant point (or points) based on a number of things, but especially, what about the story woke us up. Sometimes those elements were clear, and sometimes they seemed hidden, denied, or ignored. After identifying a koan's main point(s), we left the contributor's personal context behind and made the case our own, doing what we've done with classical koans: sinking into various aspects, wrestling with them, becoming the koan ourselves. The more we open ourselves up to a particular aspect of a koan, the greater our capacity for befriending that aspect in our daily life, including those aspects that may initially seem beyond our capacity. In that way, koans become portals of awakening into the fullness of human experience.

Of course, someone else might have focused on other elements of the story with which to grapple. A koan is like a room in a house: how you work on it changes depending on where in the room you stand. Working in this way could also lead you to question the very nature of the room, the house, the ground it sits on, and beyond.

How do householders, lucky to see a teacher once a week and do a few retreats a year, work on these koans? How do they make modern, everyday life situations a koan practice—a colicky baby keeping you up all day and night, an upstairs neighbor who's homophobic, a child tragically killed, the termination of a job? Is there a reference point, something to return to time and time again? Can we reach beyond what we already know, trusting and radically accepting the life we're given, calling nothing right or wrong or fair or unfair, appreciating the uniqueness of each moment of the situation as a blessing to penetrate and, finally, even appreciate?

"Realize your life as koan," Taizan Maezumi said.

What are you waiting for? Plunge in!

Eve Myonen Marko
Wendy Egyoku Nakao

HOME

———

ENSHO:
The Circle of Completion

———

Mother, mother, where are you?
All my life I am longing for you.
How can I ever feel complete?
Please, please, tell me what to do.

KOAN

Ensho's mother died when he was not quite two years old. It was a loss he felt throughout his life—this intense ache for the mother he would never know. One day, seventy years after her death, his mother's ashes were returned to the family. Ensho held the ashes in his hands and then gently scattered them on the ground. *Now I know you!* He then lowered his body onto the earth in a deep bow, three times.

Why did Ensho bow?

REFLECTION

As Ensho grew into adulthood, he felt deep in his being that something precious and fundamental was missing. Throughout his life, he ached for a mother he would never know. He tried many different things to address this suffering: he meditated but his body trembled, he engaged in various therapies, but resolution escaped him, and he pursued alternative energy treatments with only temporary relief. One day, in the midst of a deep spiritual crisis, he met his Zen teacher.

When Ensho formally took refuge in the Buddha Way, he was given the name *EnSho*, which means *Circle of Completion*. Through the gift of this name, his teacher pointed to a spiritual truth that Ensho himself was a circle of completion in which everything, including his mother's death and the suffering that followed, is a complete circle. How do you live this completeness when what you experience is unresolved suffering?

Spiritual teachers say that, fundamentally, you are complete and whole just as you are. And yet, there seems to be *something missing*—and the pain of *something missing* can propel you on a spiritual quest for completion.

What does it mean to be a circle of completion? Zen masters are fond of drawing empty circles that point to an essential truth: Life is intrinsically empty. The matter of birth and death is such a circle—not a void, but empty of any fixed reference point in the great round of life. The essential nature of life is fluid, and yet, everything is totally as it is and cannot be otherwise. Can you accept this?

Zen Master Dogen said that life and death is the life of the Buddha.[3] Every activity and circumstance of your life—no matter

4

how painful—is the life of a buddha. It is painful to want things to be other than they are—this pain, too, is a circle of completion. Can you stop striving to want things to be other than they are and let everything be as it is?

One day, like a bolt out of the past, Ensho's mother's ashes were unexpectedly returned to him seventy years after her death. The circle of completion moves in mysterious ways, or perhaps it seems so because we lack the sight to see its intricate and timeless workings. Zen Master Unmon said, "The whole world is medicine."

In this mysterious way, Ensho's mother came back to him; her son came back to her, too, just not in ways expected or imagined. In that moment, Ensho's being resonated: *Now I know you!* Tell me, what did Ensho realize? He found a beautiful wooded spot, held the sparse ashes in his hands, and gently scattered them on the earth. He lowered himself onto the ground; first his knees, then his elbows, and finally his forehead touched the warm earth. In this manner, he bowed three times.

Later, upon hearing of this, his teacher said, "I bow nine times."

Unmon said: "The whole world is medicine." How do you understand this? How will you use it?

YAKUSHI:
The Woman I Love

The Diamond Sutra says:
"As a lamp, a cataract, a star in space,
an illusion, a dewdrop, a bubble,
a dream, a cloud, a flash of lightning—
view all created things like this."[4]
Oh, yeah? So who do you love?

KOAN

Yakushi has been married to the same woman for years. They
share many things, including a large family, a home, a meditation
room, and a meditation practice. They also help out refugees who
have settled in the city where they live. Yakushi is aware that
many people envy him his marriage. Nevertheless, the koan he
has worked with over many years is: Why do I hate the woman
I love?

REFLECTION

Isn't it amazing how intimate love and hate are? It feels as though only a hairsbreadth separates the two. How else can you explain that you can love one person so much one day, and then hate the same person the next day, even the next hour?

No matter how loving we are with each other, no matter how strong the attraction, our relationship needs the garden beyond right and wrong, beyond *I love you/I hate you, this is great/this is awful*. It's the place not of opposites but of openness and curiosity, in which we tenderly feel not just the space between us but the space that *is* us.

> *On the mountain tonight, the full moon*
> *faces the full sun. Now could be the moment*
> *when we fall apart, or we become whole.*[5]

Becoming whole is good. Falling apart may also be good. When we fall apart, so do the mental and emotional constructs with which we experience the world. Do you notice how often, when you look at someone, you look *for* something? It's not different from looking out the window to see what the weather's like. You scan the sky, the clouds, the light. Something else may jump at you, but when you look for something you miss almost everything else.

Similarly, when we say that we see someone, are we actually seeing our loved one, or are we scanning for something, like attention, love, or acknowledgment? *Is he paying attention to me? Is she really listening or is she busy with something else? Is she really the woman I love?* If we find what we're looking for, don't we

7

love our husband or wife? And when we don't find it, don't we hate that same person? When was the last time you looked at your partner unconditionally, surrendering to his/her *as-s/he-is-ness* instead of secretly looking for what will satisfy you?

Whether we've lived together for one week or fifty years, there must always be that space of curiosity and openness, of looking at the person sitting across from me and asking the question for the thousandth time: *Who are you, really?*

And then, just wait. Don't rush to come up with a new name or label. Can you pay attention to him/her without looking for anything, relaxed and uncritical, wide open and curious? Rather than seeing your loved one, can you let yourself be seen?

In the Gospel of John, Jesus says: "And whoever sees me sees him who sent me."[6]

What kind of seeing is that?

———

When you look at the person you love, what are you really looking for? What happens when you find it or don't find it? What happens when you finally stop looking for treasure?

LAURIE:

This. Is. It!

When sharp thorns prick you, go straight on.
When prodded relentlessly, go straight on.
When your partner doesn't get you, go straight on.
When you come to a crossroad, take it!

KOAN

Laurie and Cathy were retired. Cathy did not hesitate to show her disdain for the time that Laurie spent "down there" at the Zen Center. Each time Laurie would leave the house, Cathy, from her perch on the sofa, would say, "There she goes down there again."

One Friday evening, Laurie, laden with luggage from her days away, crossed the threshold into the house. Cathy, still sitting on the sofa, asked, "Well, Laurie, have you found the meaning of life yet?"

Without hesitation, Laurie replied, "Yes, Cathy: This. Is. It!"

Cathy was silent.

REFLECTION

The way of Zen is indeed mysterious, its practice even more so to those who are not so inclined. Have you ever fallen short when you tried to explain why you practice Zen or any spiritual practice, sometimes sounding even more self-absorbed than usual? It can be so challenging to your partner when the way-seeking heart arises. Until, that is, your practice takes root and you become a better partner.

There is a famous Zen koan about an old woman who sold tea alongside the path to Mt. Tai, the home of Manjushri Bodhisattva, the exemplar of the highest wisdom. Whenever a monk would stop for tea, he would ask the old woman, "Which is the way to Mt. Tai?" She would reply, "Go straight ahead." After the monk took several steps, she would comment out loud so that he could hear her, "A fine young monk, but he, too, goes that way again."[7]

Who is the "old woman" in your life? Put aside for a time whether you think she or he is enlightened or not. The "old woman" in Laurie's house would prod her, "There she goes down there again to the Zen Center." How many of you have heard these kinds of remarks from your partner? *There he goes again, and me, look, I am home taking care of the kids, doing the yard work, and washing his clothes.*

What was Laurie seeking? What are you seeking? One might think that for Laurie, retired with a comfortable income and her own home, there would be no need to seek for anything more. Certainly her partner thought so. So what propels one person to sit on a meditation cushion for hours and another to sit on the sofa all day? Which one are you? How did you become as you are?

There is a constant dance between people who live together as a couple, each person a unique individual yet intimately inter-twined, navigating daily life together. In monastic life, monks and nuns forego singular relationships of husband, wife, or significant other. A householder, on the other hand, positions herself in inti-mate relationship with another person, within a community of family and friends.

We never know how our lives will unfold; there are no guar-antees in life other than birth, old age, illness, and death. Even the best-laid plans go awry. Laurie's way-seeking heart did not arise until after she retired from a job of forty years. When the seeking heart stirs, you are compelled to follow—there is no explaining it to anyone. When ignored, your dis-ease only intensifies. Of course, when attended to, your dis-ease also intensifies for there is no escaping the call to fulfill this deepest of desires to come home to yourself.

How do you navigate this world of relationship when the way-seeking mind arises so strongly inside? The old woman said, "Go straight ahead." But what is straight ahead in the midst of relationships? Can you navigate your way through the thicket of expectations and preferences and still attend to your partner's needs or to the needs of the relationship? Can you find the way to the heart of this life—to where the all-inclusive heart of the Bodhisattva of Nondual Wisdom resides—in the midst of the complexities of the life you are living?

As she plunged deeper into meditation, Laurie learned to tra-verse the thicket of who she was and to come to peace within herself. You could say that her inner old woman had been satis-fied. But as there was no letup at home, she had to wrestle with the "old woman" sitting on her sofa. Finally, her defenses and resentments considerably softened, she found herself in a healing acceptance of her partner and their situation together. And so it was that one night when Laurie stepped through the threshold of their abode and the "old woman" asked again, "So, Laurie, have you found the true meaning of life yet?" Laurie responded from the depths of this mystery, "Yes! This. Is. It."

This. Is. It!

Can you make such a confident declaration?

What role does your partner play in your practice? It is said that the present circumstances of your life are the perfect situation for practice. How do you see this?

———

Nena Cares for Her Brother

———

When you let go, where does it go?
When there is nowhere to go, what then?
When a mountain walks along a stream,
Bathe your feet in the cool waters.

KOAN

Nena's beloved brother had great promise as an intellectual and was the star of her family, but he did not realize his potential. He had a lifelong heroin addiction that was destroying him. He was basically Nena's dependent. Seeking help for him, she constantly asked therapists, family members, and friends, "What should I do? What should I do?"

Many people advised her by saying, "Cut him out of your life." Was that the answer?

REFLECTION

A Zen koan asks of us: "Move a mountain."[8]

What is the mountain?

A householder's life is lived in the midst of familial relationships, and for Nena, it was her challenging relationship with her troubled brother. She was terribly angry about her brother's wasted potential, called on to clean up his messes and not getting any credit from his friends for basically keeping him alive. Trying to help her brother was like moving a mountain, trying to get him to do something that he himself would or could not do. Her struggle was a long, hard slog up and down the mountain of self-doubt, anger, resentment, and fear. *What if I make a mistake? What if I don't find the right thing to do?* She knew that her bond with him was unbreakable, so the advice to cut him out of her life did not ring true to her. In her dogged determination to help her brother, Nena faced the mountain of herself.

What do you do when there are no solutions?

In Zen practice, you are called upon to do the hardest thing in the midst of suffering: sit like an immovable mountain. Sit still in the deep of yourself and listen. It takes endurance and great patience to sit unmovable in the midst of suffering without answers. Sometimes when we sit in meditation we fall asleep immediately. Sometimes thoughts churn up the mud and muck of our worries and anxieties like a rushing river. How in the world, you might ask, do I listen to myself in the midst of chaos when I can barely stay attentive?

My root teacher often said, "Poco a poco, little by little." Little by little, resistances wear down, hard edges soften, the self empties out. Nena experienced a gradual wearing down of the solid edges of inner conflict. She learned the wisdom of letting her brother be who he was and not trying to save him or change him. *Letting go* and *cutting out* are not the same. Nena gradually let go of the idea of what is an acceptable life. She set limits on her own rescuing behavior and came to peace in their relationship. Her brother noticed the change, too. She came to enjoy the fruits of mountain moving—peace, acceptance, and a way of caring for herself and her brother that was a blessing to both.

The more you listen to mountains, the more you meet the mountain within. It is amazing what you can hear: the subtle sounds, the nuanced echoes, the infinite possibilities that mountains give birth to. You learn that you do not need to fill the open space and silence of the mountain. Each breath is a breath of emptying; each step is a step of emptying. Leave aside your ideas and concepts; leave aside wanting things to be a certain way. Give up your need to fix another person or situation; let go of control.

My root teacher, whose name, Taizan, means *Great Mountain*, would often say, "Be unattached in the midst of attachments." As householders we delve into this teaching daily. What does unattached look like? Rigid and uptight? Unsentimental? Cold and uncaring, above the fray? Are you fashioning yourself into your idea of what an unattached person should be in the midst of the daily rough and tumble? My teacher said, "Be who you are, not who you think you should be, but who you truly are." What do you need to unlearn?

Nena's body-wisdom told her that cutting out her brother from her life was not the answer. There was no need to override herself with others' opinions and advice, or with her own self-judgments and habitual self-criticism. No matter the difficulties of the living relationship with her brother, the essential connection could never be severed. She could not un-brother him. This is the heart of moving mountains: to plunge into the intimacy of connection and be led by the heart song.

What action arises from emptying out and listening deeply? This unqualified experience, a response unique to you yourself, can only be known by you.

Listen!

Listen!

———

How do you bear witness to the unbearable? Can you trust in not knowing what to do, out of which your own wisdom can arise?

JUDITH:

Older Sister Mirror

"Mirror, mirror, on the wall, who's the fairest one of all?"
"You think there's two of you?"

KOAN

After fifteen years of being away, Jane visited her older sister, who lived on the opposite side of the world. A minute or two into her visit, Jane started breastfeeding her baby and talked about the advantages of breastfeeding while traveling. Her sister's response was immediate and familiar: "Be quiet! You don't know anything about it."

REFLECTION

Jane described her shocked reply from all those years ago: *But I do. I have years of experience; my children are alive, rosy, creative, and content. It is you who don't know anything! How arrogant you are, how dismissive, how judgmental! You have always put me down and been so confident in your superiority.*

Now she laughs at her outrage from long ago, but the question remains: How do we respond when someone speaks down to us, treating us with hostility or condescension? We might reciprocate, or else take refuge in a testy, resentful silence. Or else we might try to circumvent all this unpleasantness by denying what comes up, particularly our own feelings.

This last response is the way many spiritual practitioners choose to go: *It doesn't matter what she says, I'm forgiving her even as she speaks. I'm just letting it go. It's only my ego getting hurt, so it doesn't matter.*

Everything matters. When something grates inside, and we deny it or wish it would disappear, it's like saying that it doesn't matter if my left thumb hurts or the small bone in my kneecap is sore.

The One Body manifests in a twitch of a muscle, the blink of an eye, a scuffed elbow, the metallic taste of vitriol that we swallow down. Nothing is to be rejected. Every moment reveals the One Body in action: a child joyfully eating ice cream, a family killed by a drunk driver, a fish struggling in the sand, a faded rose, a leaf blowing in the wind, or a person belittling me. Seeing this clearly, why respond with judgment, sharpness, or denial?

Nevertheless, some of the most difficult moments of our lives occur when we're reprimanded, blamed, or disparaged. They bring up the old past when we were children being scolded and reproached, and there wasn't much we could do about it. Now we're older—and there still isn't much that we can do about it. We can talk back, we can hide, we can deny our feelings.

Or we can pay attention, set aside our old history of grievances and angers, and be fully present now. When we do that, when we're in the space of not-knowing, we can explore this challenging and very alive moment with some tenderness and even humor. We bear witness not just to the person admonishing us but also to our own reactions: Notice our body, the eyes dilated with anger, the lips flattened into a thin line of resentment. Notice the person so easily threatened when faced with difference, the unexpected jab, and the quick, aggressive verbal reaction: *But I do know something about it. It's you who knows nothing!*

Some tell you to remember what you have in common: *You're sisters! You're from the same family!* A Zen teacher may suggest that you explore what is beyond opposites and commonality, which is precisely this moment, ripe with dissension, and also of infinite fullness, beyond the taking of sides, beyond the self-justifying and other-vilifying, and also beyond self-abnegation or hiding.

Living the moment in this way is a tremendous act of letting go and dwelling in not-knowing. But can you let go enough to really let go? Can you feel the quivering energy in the room, the vibrancy of the Whole manifesting in two opposing forces, two opposing energies?

"Sell your cleverness," Rumi writes, "and buy bewilderment."[9]

"Be quiet! You don't know anything about it." Funny enough, that's exactly the space we'd like to create, of inquiry and being completely open. What can I say or do that will invite the other person to enter it with me, to let go of a long-held agenda and ask with full-hearted curiosity: *What is happening here? What is this about?* You're not being asked to agree, just to be a nosy visitor who wonders about everything in the house you're visiting, including the disarray in the bedroom and the unwashed dishes in the sink.

We may discover that, in the end, the most intimate thing is not agreement or seeing eye to eye, not even reconciliation and peace, but dropping further and further into *don't know*.

———

What happens when you have a conversation with a family member you've known all your life? Are you repeating scripts from the past? Do you know what s/he is going to say ahead of time? What does it take to really listen?

MYOGETSU:

Sitting in Silence

In the midst of the pots and pans,
The demanding day job, the stresses of daily living—
There is a matter of extraordinary wonder.
What is it?

KOAN

Myogetsu was eager to do more sitting meditation at home. Her husband liked to sit quietly but they did not sit together.

One evening she said to him, "You know, we should sit in meditation together. So much is communicated in silence. Perhaps we can spend fifteen minutes sitting quietly together on a Saturday morning."

"Let's spend two hours!" he replied enthusiastically.

REFLECTION

Myogetsu's life was full of activity: her daytime job, her many grandchildren, her household tasks, and caring for her mother-in-law. She had yearned to return to sitting meditation with a group, but the death of her adult daughter and the needs that followed filled her days. When things settled down, she was at last able to go to the Zen Center to sit together with the sangha. But the Zen Center was far away from her home and she yearned to sit at home, not just by herself, but also with her husband.

How about you?

There is a koan about the famous Tang Dynasty Zen Master Pai Chang. A monk asks him, "What is the matter of extraordinary wonder?" Master Pai Chang responds, "Sitting alone on Ta Hsiung Mountain."[10] Doesn't this conjure up an image of a solitary person sitting majestically in meditation on the mountaintop, removed from the fray of everyday activities?

Do you feel sometimes that sitting alone at home is not enough? Tell me, where is Ta Hsiung Mountain right now?

People who develop a sitting practice on their own often find that it is an adjustment to sit together with others in the zendo, the community meditation hall. They report feeling more self-conscious, as though the presence of others is an unwelcome distraction. Then there are those who cannot sit alone and depend on others sitting with them. What does your sitting meditation depend upon? Regardless of what your conditions are for meditation, ask yourself this question: Is your sense of self hardened, or are you emptying out and experiencing a heart opening to life just as it is, wherever it is?

How deeply can you practice at home?

You can feel the unique energy of meditation in the zendo because people have sat there for years; you can develop the same energy field in your home when you consistently meditate at home. What would your meditation space look like? Perhaps the space would be uncluttered, reminding you to empty your heart-mind of clutter. Perhaps the space faces a wall, reminding you to see beyond the walls you have built in your life. Perhaps the space has a bowl of water, reminding you of the nature of water: fluid, not resisting, life giving. Or perhaps it is next to your child's bed at night.

Myogetsu yearned to share silence with her husband. She was not asking him to sit in the meditation posture that she was accustomed to, but to simply sit as he wished and be in silence together. How about a couple sharing silence together—not the resentment-filled silence of unresolved conflicts, but the rich silence of two heart-minds in tune with what is beyond *Myogetsu* and *husband*?

What and where is this beyond?

When the Chinese Zen master Yaoshan was sitting in meditation, a monk asked him, "In sitting meditation, what do you think?" Yaoshan replied, "Think not thinking." The monk asked further, "How do you think not thinking?" Yaoshan responded, "Beyond thinking."[11] How about going to this place of *beyond thinking* together with someone sharing your household, right in the midst of the house? In other words, can you meet beyond your thoughts, beyond your busy, thinking minds? Beyond what you like and dislike about each other?

Myogetsu said, "So much is communicated in silence." This is a silence of total receptivity. What communication does not rely on thoughts, words, or touch? What is shared or exchanged when two people just sit in silence, breathing the same air in the same room together, attuning to each other's entire being-ness? In the intimacy of silence and shared energy, aren't all things thoroughly as they are: whole, complete, lacking nothing? What is this silence before your likes and dislikes arise?

Is it even possible to ever *sit alone*?

Myogetsu's husband replied, "Let's spend two hours!" What an eager fellow; he already knows the sublime gift of silence. What a way to honor one's spouse by sitting side by side, dropping self-centeredness, and allowing hearts to blossom together. When the meditation ends, for a moment you are not one and not two; everything is infused with wonder.

If your spouse is not so inclined, do not despair. After all, when the monk bowed low in gratitude upon hearing Master Pai Chang's response, the Master hit him: *Whop!* This most wonderful thing in the world is not exclusive to monks or mountaintops, sitting spouses or sitting by oneself, or whatever ideas you are forming about it.

Right here, right now, in your own being, in your very own household, there is a matter of most extraordinary wonder. It pervades the walls and windows, the carpets and curtains, the cups and saucers.

Do you see?

Whop!

Even when you are alone, what is communicated in silence? Right here, right now is the place of extraordinary wonder. How do you see it?

MARY:

The Retch

I don't like this sound; I like that sound.
When caught in the snare of likes and dislikes,
Uuuuuurrrrreeeetttch!

KOAN

A thin apartment wall separated Mary's bedroom from her new neighbor, whom she had yet to meet. Each morning, the neighbor woke up and retched. His incessant hacking felt like it was right in Mary's ear. She judged him harshly, derisively nicknaming him "the Retch."

As it happens, Mary's meditation place was located in the corner of her bedroom close to the wall she shared with "the Retch." Although she usually sat zazen well before her neighbor woke up, one morning he got up while she was sitting and started to retch loudly as though he was about to vomit out his innards.

But this morning, Mary was already in a state of expansive stillness and silence. The retching entered her being as unfiltered sound.

"Someone is suffering," she said. Compassion for him arose spontaneously.

REFLECTION

Awakening happens through the senses—the portals of eyes, ears, nose, tongue, body, and mind.[12] Of these, awakening through hearing is the most commonly recorded instance. Kyogen awakened at the sound of a pebble hitting bamboo, Sei-Kenko of Cho awakened upon hearing the thunder strike, and Ching Ch'ing awakened at the sound of raindrops. In that moment, there was just sound: everything dropped away—no cause of sound, no one to hear a sound, no hearing. There was just the *tok* of the bamboo, the *plop, plop* of raindrops, or the deafening *crraaakkkzzz!* of thunder.

There are many koans about being one with sound: *Stop the sound of the distant temple bell, the sound of one hand clapping,* or *the sound of MU.* Here, there is the sound of someone retching. Where I practice in Los Angeles, we frequently hear the song "Turkey in the Straw" played continually by the neighborhood ice cream truck or the blaring *whoowheewhoowhee* of emergency vehicles speeding by. I often tell my students, "Once you truly become one with sound, including what you may dismiss as noise, sound will never bother you again." You can disappear instantly into sound.

The universe offers up so many sounds—how do you hear them? You can call it noise, a disturbance, or an irritating distraction. You can dismiss it as an interference that diminishes your meditation practice. So often meditation students tell me that the street noise is distracting them from their meditation. Laughing,

I ask, "Where is the quiet?" Can you find the quiet in the sound? The Chinese have a marvelous saying: *The great hermit lives in the city.* Yes!

There is no way to know when awakening will happen—it just does. Sometimes you may think *If I sit long enough, if I do enough retreats, or if I spend more time in the zendo than with my family, this will cause me to awaken.* But, in fact, life is always happening, your senses are always functioning, and the conditions for awakening are always present.

Mary had developed a daily routine of sitting in a corner of her bedroom. Spaciousness and stability had been taking root within her, though she was not acutely aware of this. Led deep into a thicket of thoughts about what her neighbor was like, she continued calling her neighbor "the Retch" though they had never met in person. Perhaps you recognize this kind of rut of your conditioned mind, which is hard-wired to pass judgments and create scenarios rather than investigating the thing directly. Even as you become more aware of this tendency, you may find it difficult to reverse.

One morning, as Mary sat, a sound came into being—an unfiltered sound, before thought and perception, and before a twisted tale about the sound could arise. Instead of her usual reaction and story about "the Retch," for a moment she became *uuurrreeettch* itself and recognized it as the sound of someone suffering. In the stillness and silence, permeated with a sense of this suffering, she felt the spontaneous arising of compassion towards her neighbor.

In the stillness of meditation, a sound is just a sound. The Great Being of Compassion, Kanzeon (better known as Kwan Yin), is called the *One Who Hears the Sounds of the World.* Who is this Great Being? Manifest her now!

———

When you become one with a sound, where do you go? The sound of suffering is beyond likes and dislikes. What does suffering sound like? How do you respond to it?

DAIAN:
The Climbing Rose Vine

When vines entangle you, it is impossible to move.
When thorns prick your skin, nothing eases the pain.
When help is not available, how will you free yourself?
When the whole universe laughs, are you laughing too?

KOAN

One day Daian was carefully pruning the climbing red rose vine that he had trained to grow vertically up the water drain in the front of his house. As he stood on tiptoes on an old stump, the stump came apart right under him. The vines and thorns grabbed his legs and arms and held him there. He could not move. As he was suspended in the vines, he laughed and laughed, and asked, "Where was I before, so that I know where I am now?"

REFLECTION

How do you know when you are fully present?

Sometimes you may be lost in thoughts or feelings. At other times you may feel present, but when you look closely you see that you are unaware of many things right before you. When the stump collapsed underneath him, Daian wondered, "Where was I before so that I know where I am now?" After all, had he not been present while carefully pruning the rose vine? Thinking you are present is not the same as being present—being totally present as red roses, thorns, and rotted stumps.

It's useful to know the foundation on which you stand. Given that everything is ever-changing, is there any solid ground anywhere? People anchor themselves to various things: a retirement savings account, being surrounded by family, having a house to call home. A spiritual practitioner knows, however, that as much comfort as such circumstances may bring, none of these are truly secure because everything is in constant flux. That which you think is solid is, in fact, decaying as you read these words.

When entangled vines wrap themselves around you and the thorns of life stick into you, what foundation can you rely on? What are you counting on? A friend of mine used his breath as his foundation, but when he developed a pulmonary illness, breathing was no longer reliable. Another person grounded his wellbeing in healthy living, but when he was diagnosed with a heart condition he became disillusioned. My father relied on the stability of a lifelong marriage, but after his wife, my mother, died, he ended his life. Is there any spiritual practice that will give you enough resilience so that no matter how much you are held down by entangling vines and pricked by thorns, you will find the resources to endure?

The big life transitions shock us into the present moment, much like when Daian fell into the climbing rose vine. How about in the ongoing everydayness of life when it is easy to fall into a dull complacency without even realizing it? What wakes you up? To plunge into the present, as Daian was plunged into the vines, is to directly experience NOW. You may think that it takes a lot of effort to be present, but it is as easy as falling off a stump. When Daian could not move within the vines, he surrendered to NOW. The present is *as is*. You can never not be in it, and yet you must plunge in!

For Daian, the present was being pricked by thorns and entangled in a vine. He laughed and laughed. *Here I am!* Few experiences in life are as totally selfless as spontaneous, unstoppable laughter. But tell me, what is so damn funny? If you can truly respond to this, your suffering is at an end.

———

What is the laugh that resounds throughout the whole universe? Where are you standing now? In a life which is ever changing, where do you place your feet?

31

GEMMON:
Shadows

How to Answer a Knock on the Door
Steps:
Take precautions beforehand:
    Install a security camera.
    Install an intercom speaker system.
    Get a secure door chain if you don't already have one.
    Get a dog.[13]

KOAN

My parents' shadows are knocking at the door. Shall I open it or lock it shut?

REFLECTION

    Knock, knock!
    Who's there?
    Euro.

Euro who?
Eurolways doing something wrong!

Maybe we like jokes that start with *Knock, knock!* because shadows seem to knock on the doors of our mind all the time: memories of our family, of our parents and grandparents long gone, of our children when they were young, of ourselves when we were young. It doesn't matter who's dead and who's alive; when they knock, they're present, right here, right now.

Do I open the door or do I close it?

They knocked on my door my whole life. The decisions are always edgy between setting boundaries and being open; being the rebel, the obedient child, or the healthy adult I am now.

As different as we are, most of us follow a pretty set formula when we think of our past: *I was born in ____. My parents were ____ and ____; my siblings were ____ and ____. My childhood was ____ and also ____. When I was a teenager I ____. When I grew up I did ____, then ____. As a result of all this, I became ____ and ____.*

Isn't it practically the same script for all of us? Even though we know that nothing is that simple, we believe this formula. We believe this scrawny story.

If you cast a big enough light on your life, you'll see that there's nothing in the universe that isn't included and that hasn't influenced you in some way. Realizing that, our grasp on the formula becomes more tenuous. We clutch at our story a little more lightly, maybe a little more tenderly.

But even when we do that: *Knock, knock!* A sharp-edged memory arises and threatens to take over. We can weave it into something big and enticing. We can also leave it alone, watch it come and go, never pretend it's not there and at the same time not make it drama. It disappears by itself, but sometimes returns another day—*Knock, knock!*—and we get to do this again, and again.

Over time we might feel the pain dribbling away like water; what remains is more like a wetness that has been absorbed, leaving only a moist residue.

When we practice out of not-knowing, we work in the present moment, not in the past where we're often victims and almost always right. *Knock, knock! Who's there?* Is it really your parents from beyond the grave, or is it you? Feel your breath this moment, the sensation of air on your skin, the floor under your feet, the slant of afternoon sun on the wall. Your stories from the past are here right now, and that means that the voices are all yours, too—including those of your parents. Including the *Knock, knock!* on the door.

When you bear witness from the present moment, you experience this moment as all you. That includes past generations of your family and your ancestors. They're inescapably there in your body-mind.

Isn't that a switch? How often do we experience family bonds as chains that enslave us? How often do we wish to shake off our family history altogether? Some of us actually rush off to Zen centers for precisely that reason. And what do we find when we start to practice? That our family is us. That our family history is as much a part of us as the physical molecules that make up our body.

What do you do with your body? You take care of it. You feed it, clothe it, and attend to it. You treat it as you'd treat yourself, because it is yourself.

Buddhism is a very practical tradition. It doesn't ask what's true, it asks what works, i.e., what will relieve our suffering. Another way of saying that is: How do we make everything workable? Opening the door to the knocking of your parents is workable when you can do this with attention and care. It can result in taking more responsibility for your life. It can also result in recognizing and appreciating your personal lineage, your ancestors, and the many gifts you have received from them.

Not letting your parents in is also workable, maybe because it's time to walk the dog or do some meditation, and maybe, too, because it's not so interesting anymore.

———

Knock, knock! Who is knocking? Who is the doorman or doorwoman? And is the door solid, or is it a gateless gate?

———— ⬥ ————

CLEMENS:
The Shit Abides

———— ⬥ ————

"You're always like this!
You never do that!
Always! Never! Always! Never!"
Ahhh, lovebirds!

KOAN

Clemens, drowning in love and rancor, wonders: How can I enjoy a relationship with my loved one when we're both caught in a cage full of shit? Though the cage's windows and doors are wide open, the excrement never seems to leave the room.

REFLECTION

A friend of mine, another Zen teacher, cleans his desk and leaves it neat and immaculate at the end of each day. My desk has piles of books, notebooks, and papers, day and night; each week I move some piles around, dust around them, and move them back.

Aren't relationships more like my desk than my friend's? In fact, aren't they a lot like birdcages? There is song all day, accompanied by bird excrement. At the end of the day we remove the dirty paper bottom stained by husks of seeds and bird waste, replace the paper, cover the cage so that the bird will sleep, and the next day song and shit start all over again. This goes on even in the most mature and happiest of marriages.

Zen teaches that we are all empty of a permanent, autonomous self; that the essence of who we are is relational, co-arising with everything else in the world. It's not that nothing exists— we certainly have personality traits and a distinctive approach to life—but those characteristics are fluid and dynamic, not to be pinpointed and nailed down. They are our song, the bass and treble of our lives, endlessly creating new melodies. Sometimes they are harmonious and sometimes they are atonal, even dissonant. In the latter case, we often say they sound terrible, in fact like shit.

Isn't that the way we listen to the songs of the people around us—family members, friends, and especially the person we love? In our mind, we freeze their ever-changing song into a movie theme, the same melody with only a few variations, and we call that movie theme *him* and *her*. We create stories, impressions, and thumbnail descriptions of them that feel permanent and clear, cutting them down to a graspable size. But is that who they really are? Is that who we really are?

I can only inquire who I am at this moment. Who is that *I* now living with a man or woman whom I love? A person, an energy, a moment? And who is that *him* or *her* whom I love but at whom I am very angry right now? Anytime you think you know who that person is, you're already wrong because the moment has changed, circumstances are different, so you, she, and he are different. No one is a fixed quantity, so your opinion can't be fixed, either.

"Mom, I always love to hear your voice," I said to my far-away mother on the phone once. "You know," she responded, "it depends on the ear." In my ear, her voice was a lilting song; in someone else's, it was a dirge, a whine, or even a screech.

Life is alive and dynamic. Clinging to a fixed opinion about someone—*you're always complaining, you never do what you say you'll do*—is like taking a person's free, sprawling energy and trying to cage it up with your opinions. When you do that, don't you cage yourself up, too? Don't you cage up your relationship?

With lovebirds in a cage, comes the evening, and we clean up the bird waste by changing the paper bottom. How do you clean up the waste, day by day, in a relationship? By letting go of our fixed opinions about the person we love, we find that our labels become less definitive, more fluid. When we open up our heart, our attitude changes into one of curiosity and inquiry: *What is this?*

It can be song, screech, and everything in between. And since it moves and changes all the time, it can become all these things in a short space of time. What's the most we can say? At this moment it's this way.

But the next moment? And the one after that?

———

What do you do with the trash in your relationship? Opening up the doors and windows helps, but what are you doing with your opinions?

SELENA:
Unqualified

This way won't do,
That way won't do.
Not this way won't do,
Not that way won't do.
Help!

KOAN

Upon moving to Los Angeles, Selena and her wife had found their ideal apartment and eagerly looked forward to settling into married life. But upon moving in, they discovered that their upstairs neighbor stomped on their bedroom ceiling all night, delivering a litany of racist, sexist, and homophobic declarations. Selena became deeply entangled in her thoughts about him, loathing him and going out of her way to avoid him. One afternoon, Selena returned home and came upon her neighbor pruning the roses in the common garden space. He called her over to him and declared: "I like your wife better than I like you."

Stunned, Selena heard herself say, "So do I."

Their eyes met, they burst into laughter and shared a high-five. Selena's defenses melted.

REFLECTION

Selena was living in her dream apartment with the woman she loved, but the upstairs neighbor's behavior challenged her in so many ways. Isn't this the way of the conditioned self? There is always an exception, that one thing that stands in the way of one's peace of mind. We can become easily fixated on the object of our dissatisfaction: *If only he were not my neighbor, life in the apartment would be perfect.* We are hard-wired to go down this path of *if only: If only I had more money, if only my husband did not have a stroke, if only my boss weren't such a jerk.*

Selena sensed that underneath his behavior and big, rough exterior, the neighbor was a good-hearted person. He, too, had expressed his dis-ease with having new neighbors that he would have to adjust to. After all, he did not hesitate to tell her how much he had liked the former neighbor. Selena had no idea how to relate to him. She was entangled in a constricting net of reactivity and did everything she could to avoid him. She qualified him by labeling him "the stomper," "the homophobe," and so on.

What does your mind wrap itself around? When have you been bound up by your reactivity—this way won't do, that way won't do—over and over again? Even when you want to affirm the connection, you simply don't know how to go about it. Instead, you double down and seem unable to connect with the common humanity you share with the other person. Selena was lost, with all her buttons pushed to the max.

In accord with her spiritual practice, Selena strived to keep an open heart and mind, to come from not-knowing instead of reactivity. But her feelings about homophobes and racists kept zeroing in on her neighbor. The more they did this, the less she was able to experience him and herself in an open, unqualified way.

This went on until one day, before she could avoid him yet again, he saw her and called her over. We've all been drawn in like that—the very person we are avoiding suddenly appears before us. It's too late to hide yourself once again. So here was Selena face-to-face with the very person whose qualities, as she saw them, made her so uncomfortable.

"I like your wife better than I like you!" he declared to her.

"Me, too!" she replied without hesitation. There was no time for her usual thought spinning, no time to retreat back into her usual mindset.

Instead, a moment of transcendence: A spark. A healthy connection. A great laugh. A high five. No more resistance. Truly, there is nothing like being shocked out of yourself.

What shifts for you in a moment like this when all pretense and qualifications fall away? His struggle and her struggle were extinguished in the immediacy of the surprise encounter. In that moment, Selena was suddenly unqualified, unconstricted, and free.

When reactivity is extinguished, how do you greet a person whose presence causes you distress? Listen deeply to yourself and watch yourself closely: go to the place beyond qualifications. Where is it?

HERMAN:
Crying

Happiness, happiness, great happiness.
Sorrow, sorrow, great sorrow.
Tears fall and the heart softens by itself.
Why does a great being cry?

KOAN

Whenever Herman returned home from a trip, his mother cried with joy from the moment she saw him. Whenever he left home again, his mother cried with sorrow. Herman was deeply embarrassed by her crying, especially when she cried at the airport in front of everyone.

Each time she cried, Herman would say, "Mom, please don't cry like that. If you keep crying like that, I won't come home anymore." But still his mother cried.

One day, Herman found himself crying, too.

REFLECTION

When meditation is practiced regularly, emotions often arise unbidden. You may experience anger, sadness, loneliness, and, not infrequently, a deluge of tears.

Many students say to me, "Something is wrong with my sitting."

"Why do you say that?" I ask.

"Because I am crying," is often the response. Meditation releases emotions—it is not a dry practice. When you allow the feelings to surface in meditation, you will experience a natural releasing and cleansing. A student who cried whenever she saw me once said, "Why don't you teach me something?" I replied, "You need to cry. Your body-mind is healing itself." Crying prepares the ground for sprouting the seeds of awakening.

Meditation reveals your humanity. You learn to live in the skin of the human being that you are, doing what human beings do: feeling anger, loneliness, and sadness; laughing and crying. It all seems so wrong, so awkward, depending upon the feelings that you've repressed due to familial or cultural conditioning or the depth of trauma you've experienced. Crying is a natural and healthy human response to life.

Does crying make you uncomfortable? Do you suppress your feelings? You are in big trouble when your meditation practice has at its base an image of a serene meditator who is removed from the fray of human emotions. Can you let go of that image and find the natural place for feelings and emotions within yourself, or are you molding yourself into your image of what a meditator looks like? Where is the place for feeling in spiritual practice?

Herman was a determined and rational man who had set his sights on becoming an engineer. Although he felt deeply, he did not express his emotions freely. His mother's emotional freedom embarrassed him; he tried to change her and distance himself further from his own feelings. How about you: What is your strategy?

Zazen, sitting still and open, is deeply healing. It continually amazes me how much is revealed and released in the simple act of sitting still in receptive awareness, open to everything. Sitting is fundamentally all-encompassing: This very body-mind breathes in the whole universe and breathes out the whole universe. You yourself are being breathed by everything: Where is there for anything to be hidden? Practice allows you to not fear emotions; emotions are energy, not repressing them makes you strong and resilient.

Meditation practice gives us the gift of feeling directly, without our habitual methods of interference. Through sitting, you develop stability, spaciousness, and a disciplined attentiveness. These three qualities together enable you to sit in the midst of strong emotions without acting out or repressing them. You learn to feel directly what is arising in your body: the tightening of muscles in the abdomen, the surge of heat in the chest, the warm wetness in the eyes. The conditioned mind is quick to go into a story about what is happening. Can you interrupt your narrative and not let the story obscure the actual sensation arising in your body? Can you feel the energy directly? This is not to say that circumstances and reasons are unimportant, but rather that when you can take the backward step and just feel the experience directly in the body, your response is often more appropriate to the situation.

Herman engaged in an elaborate strategy around his mother's crying. One day, he found himself crying with his mother—a beautiful shared experience. It is one thing to cry alone in our room, quite another to cry together. I remember that after my root teacher, Taizan Maezumi Roshi, died, my dharma brother, Rabbi

Don Singer, said, "Now we know the sangha will survive because we have all cried together."

Finding himself crying with his mother, Herman realized that he did not have to try and change her. There was nothing to fix. As he realized that her tears expressed her love for him, his natural tenderness and vulnerability arose. How about for you? Tell me, how does an awakened person cry?

———

Do you experience your emotions directly as raw energy, or do you try to escape them by acting out, repressing, or telling stories about them? Do you succumb to an image of a rigid meditator who is beyond feeling?

EMMA:
Pocket of Love

Yellowed newspapers and magazines piled high.
Old clothing overflowing cardboard boxes.
Paper bags, plastic bags, gift wrapping, and bows.
Books and magazines covered with dust—
Oy vey, what state of mind is this?

KOAN

Emma was a hoarder. One night, asleep in her tiny, overstuffed apartment, she had a dream. A man was cooking a meal for her and a woman was helping her clean. Emma herself was sorting through a large stack of cards. Suddenly, she felt suffused with love. Emma said, "I am unrestricted. Why am I holding on to this stuff? There is endless possibility."

Upon waking, Emma declared out loud: "I am a pocket of love and so is everyone else." The next day while looking out the window, Emma heard the trees, grasses, and walls saying to her, "Love. Love."

She went to see her teacher and asked, "What will I do when this awareness fades away?"

Her teacher replied, "Shifting to love is as easy as smiling."

REFLECTION

Emma had lived well into her seventh decade with a nagging belief that she was not lovable. Although she had accomplished much in her life, she hid within herself and cluttered her apartment with belongings, unable to sort through them and clear them out. She had glimpses into how she came to be like this, but she felt it would be too difficult to change.

Perhaps there is a bit of a hoarder in each of us. Do you use things to create a protective barrier around you? Some people may also hoard due to a sense that they lack something essential, that there is a hole inside that nothing—not even all the love in the world—can fill. Sometimes a nagging voice saying *I am unlovable* lives within us as a whisper, at other times a shout, loud and clear.

Perhaps you, too, are consumed with an underlying fear that you are unlovable. No matter how much you have meditated, extended loving kindness to yourself and others, or done years of therapy, the sense of being unlovable persists. Perhaps you employ strategies of self-improvement or a change in circumstance, or you become the best at your job to compensate for this lack.

One night, Emma dreamed that she was whole and complete. She saw that she herself was a pocket of love. Emma's realization reminds me of the monk Seizei, who seeks to be released from a poverty-stricken spirit. He goes to Master Sozan and begs for help. Master Sozan replies, "You have already drunk three cups

47

of the finest wine and still you say that you have not moistened your lips."[14] How is it that you yourself are the finest of wines and yet you do not know it?

When you keep opting for the old habitual ruts, rerunning the stories in your head around fear, self-doubt, and self-hatred, the choice you're making reinforces your self-absorption. Instead, imagine creating a huge compost pile full of fear, self-doubt, and self-hatred. As you add these ingredients to the compost, practice accepting these qualities without indulging them as you tend and turn the pile. Do this over and over again, exerting great patience as you accept all that you are, including your broken bits and all that you are hoarding. Extend love to your brokenness. By embracing your suffering tenderly in this way, this compost pile will become a nutrient-dense conditioner for the soil of your awakening.

Emma found that resting in love was liberating, preferable by far to living in her fears and perniciously limiting thoughts. Realizing that there was fundamentally no restriction, she could continuously choose love and live it moment by moment in full acceptance of whatever arose in her life. After a while, however, Emma became worried that this love, too, would pass. "What then?" she asked her teacher. Her teacher said, "Love is as easy as smiling."

Love is always right here, right now. Shortly after her dream, Emma made a big decision: She sorted through her belongings and moved to another state to live.

Shift!

Smile!

What's in your pocket? What protective barrier do you build around yourself to keep life at bay? Show me how you turn the compost pile of broken bits!

Jackie Gives a Gift

The giver is empty,
The receiver is empty,
The gift is empty—
So why am I suffering so much?

KOAN

When Jackie was about to receive the Zen Buddhist precepts, her teacher told her that the ceremony included bows to her parents. Jackie blurted out that years ago she had sent her father a hundred dollars. Her mother had always cautioned her not to send him money because "he would only drink it." Upon receiving the money, her father bought a case of whiskey. He drank the entire case, was hospitalized, and died. Jackie spent years on a psychologist's couch over this.

Her teacher listened, gave a small nod of his head, and said, "That was giving."

Upon hearing this, Jackie was healed.

REFLECTION

With what heart do you give? With what heart do you receive?

Jackie gave her father a gift and the way he used it brought her years of anguish. The Ten Grave Zen Precepts continually remind us that not only should you yourself not drink alcohol and cloud the mind, but you are also admonished not to create an environment for others to become drunk and cloud the mind. While Jackie's guilt and sense of responsibility for her father's death were understandable, what in her teacher's response—*That was giving*—ultimately freed her from her years of anguish?

In Zen, it is said that the giver, the gift, and the receiver are all empty of any fixed sense of *you* and *me,* of expectation and fulfillment. In the realm of the intrinsic nature of life, there is no *you* who gives, no *you* who receives, and no gift that is given—there is only energy circulating. Giving based on self-interest, driven by a personal agenda, is fraught with suffering. Giving practiced unconditionally, on the other hand, aligns you with the dynamic, interdependent flow of the life force that is beyond *you* and *me.*

What does this mean for how you are giving? You would naturally consider the time, person, place, and amount in order to give an appropriate gift. Even giving in this considered way, however, requires awareness and discipline in order to detect subtle self-interest. Perhaps you are plagued with a crazy-making inner dialogue: *How will this gift make me look? What will I lose by giving this gift? Will I regret giving it?* So, tell me, how do you give with complete relinquishment? Was Jackie wrong to give her father a hundred dollars? Was a hundred dollars the wrong gift to give her father? Was her father wrong to use the gift as he did?

One day I was sitting in a restaurant when a homeless man came in and went to each table asking for change. As I watched him circle through the entire restaurant, I placed some coins on my table. When he came my way, he took the coins, we nodded to each other, and he left. A restaurant patron came up to me and yelled, "Why did you give him money? Don't you know what he is going to do with it?" "No," I replied. "I don't know what he will do with it, and I don't care, either." "What?" yelled the irate patron. "You don't care?!" He stormed away from my table in frustration and disgust. As the other diners returned to their meal, I sat there surprised at my own responses.

When does a gift become a gift—when it is given, when it is received, or when it is received and given away again? Nature is perhaps the best manifestation of relinquishment. Air circulates freely throughout the earth, rain falls equally on plants, and we absorb oxygen released by plants without inhibition. Just as your life helps to sustain the lives of others, the reverse is also true. In this continual cycle of giving and receiving, you are naturally aligned with the basis of the bodhisattva life, the perfection of giving. At what point does giving become conditional?

Can the true impact of a gift ever be known? When the young girl cow herder, Sujata, saw a suffering ascetic, she offered him a bowl of milk curds. The ascetic drank it, sat under the bodhi tree, and became enlightened, a Buddha. That gift made its journey through the next forty years of the Buddha's life as he led others to awakening. Here, now, centuries later, that bowl of milk curds continues to give life to you and me. Receiving it with gratitude and sharing it with others is the gift's journey; Jackie's teacher used it to free her. Perhaps this gift will end its journey when all beings are liberated. May it be so.

———

What expectations do you attach to giving? With what mind do you receive the offerings of others? Of life itself? Identify a transformative gift. Can you trace its journey?

CARLOS:
An Imaginary Person

Tell me what to do, please.
Make the formula easy to recall.
I want to paste it on the wall.
It must apply to all.
Whop!

KOAN

Carlos asked: "Mom, someone in our neighborhood was really mean to me today. What should I do about him?"

His mother responded: "Who is this someone? Tell me who he is. I can't give you any suggestions for an imaginary person."

Carlos had an insight.

REFLECTION

Carlos was fond of developing rules and strategies for how to conduct himself. He hoped to avoid difficulties by knowing what rules to follow. In this way, he thought, he could avoid unpleasant interactions and always know the right thing to do.

This is a common approach among those who like explicit rules, a kind of how-to manual for living. There is no risk involved: Just do this and don't do that. It's the literal approach that allows no room for the complexities in actual situations that seem too messy to deal with. Nuance and ambiguity, however, are the very nature of life.

When the precepts are studied in Zen, several approaches are taken. For example, there is the literal approach: *Do this and don't do that*. There is also the relational approach: *Do this and don't do that, depending on the circumstances*. Rules, on the other hand, are not fully alive because they are created based on past experiences. This does not mean that a rule has no value, but the question arises of whether and how it relates to a real situation right now. Fixing on a rule can disconnect you from the particularities of the actual situation you are living. Life is not a generality.

What do you do when you don't know what to do?

Once I counseled a couple in preparation for their marriage. They were rewriting the Zen Buddhist precepts into life vows that they thought best suited their relationship and hopes for their life together. They hit a snag and returned to see me. Listening to them, it became clear to me that, on the one hand, she approached life out of a clearly defined set of dos and don'ts. He, on the other hand, was comfortable dealing with ambiguity, discerning contexts and circumstances.

How are you inclined? What ties you up in knots?

Carlos's mother knew that particulars are important. That includes the nuances of every situation and the uniqueness of our personalities. People come to me, as the head teacher, to discuss a difficulty they are having with someone else in our community. These conversations often sound very much like Carlos's conversation with his mother. Their reluctance to be specific about the person or situation in question is understandable, but it often undermines my ability to respond in a direct, helpful way. After all, life situations are not hypothetical. You and the other person are particular beings with unique and specific characteristics that are best served by a willingness to engage with each other. Dumbing the situation down into an abstraction is neither skillful nor helpful.

Of course, you could reflect on your part in a troubling situation; self-reflection is, after all, a core component of spiritual life. But how much self-reflection is the right amount? I notice that people who are often inclined in this way show signs of self-absorption. There is too much "self" in their reflection. Is this true of you? There is, after all, at least one other person involved as well. How do you engage with him or her in an open and expansive way, not reducing that person to an abstraction?

Who is this other person? I recall that my Zen teacher, upon listening to his students giving dharma talks, said, "You all talk about the sameness, the essential nature of everyone. Tell me, what are you going to do about the differences? The differences are important." How will you know differences? Setting aside your projections and value judgments, tell me: Who is standing before you? This continues to be very alive for me: Where is the person coming from? What uniqueness is she bringing to the situation? How can I learn about it without judgment, but with curiosity and openness?

Bernie Glassman, founder of the Zen Peacemakers, would often say, "If you want to know oneness, you must know differences." Carlos's mother knew the wisdom of differences. She knew that life is not prescriptive and general, but rather precisely different. She did not view differences as a problem, but rather as unique expressions of life that must be recognized as such so that an appropriate response can arise. When you don't see this, you are indeed dealing with an imaginary person.

Right now, show me the difference!

———

When you react to someone, what difference or specific quality are you reacting to? When you drop your judgment about it, who is standing before you?

RAISING
CHILDREN

SALAAM:
Not Doing Enough

---

*One little, two little, three little Indians [enough
    already!]—*
*Four little, five little, six little Indians [you mean there's
    more?]—*
Seven little, eight little, nine little Indians—
HELP!

KOAN

Salaam had five little children, so she had a room where the floor
was covered with mattresses. The youngest twin babies lay next
to her so that she could nurse them whenever they felt hungry. At
the same time, she could give the middle one his bottle and keep
the two oldest very close because they needed her, too. It was
exhausting, but at least she didn't have to stand up and change
rooms each time she went from one child to another. And still she
wondered, anxiously, day and night: Am I doing enough?

REFLECTION

One woman, five young children.

Feeding, holding, changing diapers, stroking, kissing, listening, cuddling, tickling, cooing, singing, lullabying, rocking, suckling, bouncing, cooking, washing, ironing, mopping, playing, humming, cleaning, emptying dishwashers, giving baths, soaping, shopping, brushing, wiping, driving, fondling, and burping. Not to mention the husband who needs attention, the parents who wonder why you don't call more often, the retreats you can't do, the school meetings you're always late for, and the friends you never see but who tell you to take care of yourself.

How?

What do I do when I am confronted by needs without limit, claims without end? Work is never finished, and I don't get enough rest. Each night I go to bed knowing that the next day will be like this, and the day after that, and the day after that. Another mother told me, "When I open my eyes in the morning and think of what's ahead for me, I just want to crawl right back under the blanket and go to sleep."

Salaam asked: "Am I doing enough?" How do you measure *enough*? One smile from your child, five, ten? Three from each? One definition of enough might be that your children are safe, clean, fed, and sheltered. But what about attention? What about love?

What is your answer? Whatever it is, can you let it go? Can you see the fluid nature of *enough/not enough* and hold the concept loosely?

Maybe your sense of *enough* comes from reading lots of books about child-rearing. Maybe it comes out of a feeling of not getting enough from your own parents. Maybe it comes out of watching a friend raise her children, idealizing her, and deciding that you want to be like her. It doesn't matter where it comes from; what matters is *playing freely in the Pure Land*, as we say in one of our Buddhist chants. For your children, that may mean play time in the sandlot, but for parents, it means not being held captive by *enough*.

What set of criteria am I using to judge myself, preventing me from bearing witness and appreciating my efforts for what they are?

"The rush and pressure of modern life are a form, perhaps the most common form, of its innate violence. To allow oneself to be carried away by a multitude of conflicting concerns, to surrender to too many demands, to commit oneself to too many projects, to want to help everyone in everything, is to succumb to violence."[15] The Catholic contemplative and activist Thomas Merton addressed this concern to social activists, but he might as well have been talking to many of us who wish we could do more, think we should do more. Life calls out and we respond to the best of our abilities—including the creative and compassionate act of covering the floor with mattresses.

The word *overwhelm* comes from *whelm*, an old English word meaning *to cover*. When I feel overwhelmed, I feel drowned or crushed under a heavy burden that covers me and hardly lets me breathe. But what is this burden? Is it my life, or is it the concepts and ideals that I cling to?

Instead of getting stuck in the dead-end rut of asking what is enough, which implies lack, can you reframe the experience as something positive and affirming, see each moment as a complete expression of your love for this child? A room full of mattresses shows creativity, skill, and compassion at work. What a wonderful thing it can be to have all your children in one room, a space knitting everyone together! Each moment knits everything together, too, no matter how incomplete it may feel to you because of your ideas and concepts about it.

Inhabit your body-mind fully. A half-hour of fully embodied attention and presence evokes abundance and love much more than the rush of trying to cover all bases. And if you feel overwhelmed, give a sigh and return to the breath.

Having a child is not a linear addition, like adding a room to an existing house: it changes the entire house. The same with having a second child, and a third, and a fourth. How do you respond?

———

"From the beginning, nothing has been withheld," says Eihei Dogen, founder of the Soto Zen Sect. If so, what is not enough in your life? What is too much, or too little? If you think you know, go back to not-knowing.

MYOKAN:

"MOM!"

Chao-Chou's "Mu!" has nothing on children's "Mom!"
With the first, the world falls apart;
With the second, the abyss opens—
Not once but hundreds of times.
MOM! MOM! MOM! MOM!

KOAN

MOM! I don't have any clean underwear for school today!

MOM! Can we drive to the other mom's house right now and get my lacrosse stuff?

MOM! My blood sugar is low!

MOM! I missed the school bus!

MOM! Here's a daffodil I picked for you from the neighbor's garden.

REFLECTION

I love you! I hate you! I tore my sweater! I need a lift! My nose is bleeding! I'm not going to school! I love my phone! I'm not eating meat! MOM! DAD! MOM! DAD!

One thing after another, day after day after day after day.

"I used to sit every morning," one father said. "When we had kids, I'd get up earlier and earlier in the mornings to meditate and I'd cut the periods shorter and shorter. Now, if I'm lucky I sit for ten to fifteen minutes, and the kids start calling out before I finish." *What's for breakfast? Can I watch TV? The dog needs to go out! Who's taking me to soccer practice?*

When you're a parent, it's good to designate small periods of sitting rather than long ones; it's good to plan for something practical and feasible. But meditation is a practice of paying attention at each moment to what is at hand. Isn't that what you must do for the rest of the day?

Buddhist history is full of stories of monks sitting out in the freezing cold, on sharp-edged rocks or under dripping water as means of staying focused and attentive. Today Japanese Zen monks in the great temple of Eihei-ji continue to daily wash its many steps with toothbrushes, a practice that is hundreds of years old. By the same token, today's parents are called to pay attention to their children and their needs hour after hour, moment after moment, a relentless schedule of practice.

Mom! I'm coming.

Dad! I'll be right there.

Mom! I'll take you to school.

Dad! I'll make you lunch.

Don't forget, children are not the only ones to vie for our attention, everything calls out all the time. Every day the leaves call out for sun, the tree roots hunt for moisture, the birds seek out worms, the hawks hunt for other birds, our heart calls out for blood and our lungs for air.

The world calls out and the world responds. When our children are small and can't care for themselves, we care for them, but life took care of them long before they were born by providing oxygen for their lungs and an unimaginably complex system comprising trillions of cells. No matter how hard we work, we can't duplicate those efforts. Our children's needs and wants—*Where's my lunchbox? The phone is ringing! Would you read me a story?*—are the dainty sauces in a banquet that took billions of years to prepare and cook and has long been served.

That doesn't mean we don't take care of them; it is a good reminder that most of it is not really up to us.

Zen liturgical chants are usually followed by dedications, one of which goes as follows:

The absolute light, luminous throughout the whole universe, unfathomable excellence penetrating everywhere.

Whenever this devoted invocation is sent forth it is perceived and subtly answered.

Every request, every call, is perceived and subtly answered. We stand, and the floor holds us up. My finger flicks a switch and light beams across the room. I pull a handle and the door opens. Kwan Yin, the mother of compassion, is often depicted with many hands because she never stops working, and I am but one of her infinite number of hands.

My teacher and husband, Bernie Glassman, often said that if we knew ahead of time how many breaths we'd have to take in order to live to the end of our days, which can number in the hundreds of millions, some of us would feel pretty discouraged before we even started. But start we must, one breath after another, day after day after day.

In doing so, do we breathe superfast in order to get all our breathing done? Do we start to hyperventilate?

It's very common to rush in the face of many demands and multitask like crazy. My grandfather, the old rabbi from pre-Holocaust Romania, used to peer over his beard at his small, manic granddaughter and say, wagging his finger, "Not even angels can do more than one thing at a time." No matter how many demands life makes of us, in the end we can only fulfill them one at a time. Since that's all our system is designed to do, eternally trying to do more stresses us out.

Eat breakfast, wash your bowls, carry water, chop firewood. Basic Zen instructions from thirteen hundred years ago for how to fully live your life. You can try to do your tasks fast and easy, rushing from one thing to the next. Or you can take a deep breath, say *yes*, *no*, meet your child's eyes, be fully here. MOM! becomes the bell of attention, reminding you to plunge in, now.

Can you take an hour—or a half hour—each day and be fully attentive to your child? When other things come up, always bring your attention back to your child.

Sara's Laundry

Doing laundry, collecting toys, cleaning house, cooking dinner—
Are they deluded or enlightened activities?
If you think it's easy to say no, try saying yes.
Beyond no and yes, where's the Dharma Hall in a messy house?

KOAN

Sara hears her son calling from another room. "I'm coming!"

She walks down the hall and steps on a Lego piece. "Ouch!"

She turns the corner and slips on a Superman cape left on the floor. "Whoa!"

She pushes aside a large pile of laundry on the couch, sits down, looks into the eyes of her son, and has an insight.

REFLECTION

We like to organize our disorderly life into categories with names like *goals, messes, failures, successes, obstructions,* etc. While these labels help us make sense of things, even giving us a feeling of control, they isolate us more and more from the actual experience.

Ouch! and *Whoa!* remind us that we're alive. Lego pieces, with their famous ridges, are wonderfully formed not just to fit into each other but also to wake us up when we step on them: *Ouch!* I thought I was in a hurry to get to the other room to be with my son and—*Ouch!* Or else a Superman cape fortuitously causes my legs to slide and my knees to almost buckle on my way quickly to the next room: *Whoa!*

Ouch! and *Whoa!* make us forget ourselves, our thoughts, plans, and distractions, much like the hitting of the flat wooden stick used on Zen practitioners' shoulders in the meditation hall. In the ancient koans, a teacher gives a yell or a blow with his staff to get the student out of his head and into *NOW!* Doesn't taking care of your family and the home present similar opportunities? The hot water in the shower turns suddenly cold, the washing machine breaks down in the middle of the wash cycle, and the dog has an accident on the floor right after you mopped it. These experiences all pull the rug from under our assumptions and certainties, if only for an instant, before we've had time to react. In that instant we are out of our heads and really here.

How quickly do we escape the experience and rush into reactivity? How quickly do we get back into our heads?

The question isn't how to avoid a life of pitfalls and surprises, there's no avoiding that. Life is hardship, accidents, a tortuous path of unforeseen twists and turns—and it's workable. We add a large measure of unnecessary suffering through our criticism, regrets, and mournful commentary on our life: *Why did this have to happen? How could he do this to me?*

"How do you go straight on the narrow path that has ninety-nine curves?" asks a classic koan. The answer is right in the question. As Sara demonstrates, there is no curve that is not navigable. A piece of Lego, a Superman cape, heaps of laundry, an unexpected tragedy, illness, death—these are not separate from that narrow path, they *are* the narrow path. Each event can also be a gate, a promise, an opportunity for intimacy.

Niklaus Brantschen, a Swiss Jesuit and Zen teacher, was highly athletic, a mountain climber well into his seventies. When he was eighty, cancer was discovered in his body, and his entire stomach, along with a portion of his large intestine, was removed. Niklaus remained cheerful. "You know, I now have to learn how to eat in a completely different way," he marveled. "I have to eat without a stomach. Imagine eating like a bird, tiny meals many times a day. Who could imagine that at my age I would learn all this? I am very grateful for this new practice."

"Curiosity, not criticism," a friend recommended. *What is this?* rather than *How could this happen?* Our life presents us with countless opportunities for this practice.

Day by day, the parents of this world go back, again and again—not to their breath, not to *Mu* or their counting—but to their children, with complete attention and awareness. They stumble and slide over toys, exclaiming *Ouch!* as they try the overheated milk, shivering *(Brrrr!)* when they're attacked by snowballs, uttering *Ahhh!* in wonder when they see their toddler on top of the stairs eagerly waiting for them to come home. And they have an insight.

When the road zigs and zags, with stumbling blocks everywhere, can you ever reach your destination? What is your destination?

CHRISTINE:
The Calling Child

Each of us has our position; each of us has our work.
The great miracle is not stumbling out of bed when my
*   child calls*
But getting horizontal when it's time to sleep,
Vertical when I get up.

KOAN

Why do you jump up in the middle of the night when your child calls out?

REFLECTION

There are so many things we do without planning ahead of time; in fact, the great majority of our actions don't require any thinking at all. If the left foot moves forward, the right one will probably follow without any consultation between them. If a car suddenly cuts me off, my foot will usually hit the brakes automatically. I sometimes call these actions no-brainers, because we don't have to think about what to do. Similarly, our digestive system works without orders from us. As I write this, my fingers know exactly where to go on the keyboard, and when I read my words on the screen, my right arm creeps up and plants my elbow on the desk. How does it know that I like to lean my head on my palm as I read? Because it's a no-brainer.

Scientists say that these are all learned behaviors, whether dating back to a driver's ed class fifty years ago or to bits of memory stored by our DNA a couple of million years ago. But it all comes to the same thing: At each moment, action is taking place without conscious ordering or decision-making by me.

So what happens when your young child suddenly calls out in the middle of the night? You probably jump out of bed to see what's wrong. You don't pause to ask whether you should do this, whether you're not too tired, or how you will get up in the morning to go to work. Later, you might feel your exhaustion and wonder how you'll make it through the day, but the moment you hear that sudden cry, you jump out of bed.

Do you do that every time? My husband calls me when I'm in the middle of doing something; the dog whines for breakfast when I'm still in bed; a friend invites me to a movie. The situations that find me uncertain or reluctant are the ones I think about.

A friend likens it to going to the library. Some things we learn by going to the library, but many things we know how to do on our own. The questions we ask the librarian, or our consciousness, are the ones we're confused about. A homeless woman asks for a handout—what do I do? My father is developing Alzheimer's while still young—what do I do? Someone says *I love you* or *I don't love you anymore*—what do I do?

We're part of a flow of call-and-response. When we follow that flow in a natural and smooth way, unhindered, we're not fighting our thoughts or our feelings, we're not fighting ourselves; we're just doing what's in front of us without distraction.

There's a famous koan about a wind flapping a temple flag. Two monks argued about it, one saying the flag was moving and the other insisting it was the wind that was moving. Passing by, the seventh-century Chan master Huineng said, "It is neither the wind nor the flag that is moving. It is your mind that is moving."[16]

Life shows up. The wind is doing its thing, the flag does its thing, and our mind goes into a tizzy. It provides names, labels, and descriptions—*The wind is moving! No, the flag is moving!*—and then starts arguing with itself.

What confuses us? Not things in themselves, but our own feelings, judgments, and preferences, which swell like big balloons and carry us off. When the mind settles, don't you see more clearly? Doesn't the flow of activity feel natural and organic?

Some people twist themselves inside out trying to figure it all out, convinced that if they think it through long enough things will work out in the end. Life works out regardless. The question is, where are *you*? Are you living it or arguing about it in your mind?

When I lived in a poor neighborhood of southwest Yonkers, I couldn't go home without being stopped and asked for money. The story I heard most frequently was that the person needed money to buy Pampers for the baby. I never knew what to do. There were too many ingredients in the fire: ideals of giving freely, the fact that I had little money, anger towards people I was sure were conning me, awareness of the high rate of drugs and alcohol where we lived, the difficulty I had saying no.

One day I walked up the hill and, sure enough, a woman stopped me and asked for money to buy Pampers for her baby. "You're all telling me the same story every day, I don't believe a word you say!" I finally told her.

She grinned and gave me a sassy look. "Okay, but could you lend me a five?"

I looked straight back at those cocky eyes and laughed. With just a few words she'd taken me out of that cauldron of guilt and confusion and brought me right to that moment of encounter, face to face.

I can't remember if I gave her money or not, only that my laugh was a no-brainer.

———

Why do you get up at the sound of your baby? Why do you go to the door at the sound of the doorbell? Why do you put your coat on in winter? Why do you vow to save all beings?

MYOTAI:
Little Bodhisattva

A thirteen-year-old girl preaches the Dharma
Without robes, bells, and bowing.
Her arms hug, her lips curve into a smile—
How do you respond?

KOAN

Myotai was tucking in her thirteen-year-old daughter for the night.

"Oh, yum," Kai said. "You smell like meditation. I love tuck-me-ins after meditation with the community."

Myotai asked, "What do you mean, Kai?"

Kai said, "Well, first I like you, Mom, and, at the same time, I like all of the people that you sit with. Your people are my people. They just don't know it yet."

Myotai experienced a shift.

REFLECTION

How far does your meditation reach?

When Kai was hugged by her mom, who had just returned from sitting with her meditation group, she sensed that meditation is vast and wide with nothing obstructing its flow. How about you? How far do you extend?

In other words, where do you draw your boundary?

Many people identify their skin as the boundary of who they are. Others create a mind boundary by using only the rational and logical mind. Still others establish a heart boundary by including only people they prefer and excluding all those that they dislike. We identify with a boundary of some kind, and within that boundary, we experience ourselves as limited beings, armoring ourselves to protect our well-established boundaries from all that is outside. People often refer to an inside and an outside, and most of what is outside the boundary is not seen as oneself or as being even remotely related to oneself. In this way, the *other* that is *not me* is created. In doing so, a solid sense of *me, mine, and myself* is reinforced.

What happens to this view when you experience meditation?

When I started to meditate, I began to experience myself not as a separate and disconnected individual being but as part of the great dynamic net of interbeing. Rigidly-held boundaries began to dissolve, and I felt my sense of self become more porous. This net, which Buddhists call Indra's Net, has no boundary between inside and outside; it extends infinitely. Each node of the net is a connecting point reflecting and influencing every other node.

Close your eyes for a moment and imagine yourself a node in this boundless net. Of this unlimited intersecting relationship, my teacher Bernie Glassman said with a smile, "Before, there was Indra's Net; today we have the Internet." It's the same principle. Now tell me, where do you place your boundaries?

Please do not be confused. The essential no-boundary nature of life does not remove the need for healthy boundaries in everyday interactions. The key is: Is your boundary life-affirming or does it harm you or a particular person or group? For some people, cultivating healthy boundaries means learning to set them; for others, it means learning to release rigidly-held boundaries. Wherever you are on the spectrum, in the essential realm, there are no boundaries; in the relational realm, there is nothing but boundaries.

When Kai was hugged by her mother, feeling the warm, familiar touch of her skin and breathing in her smell, she felt hugged by all the energies of the people her mother had been meditating with that evening. For Kai, there was no boundary. The entire community of meditators was hugging her. She felt the boundless and all-pervading nature of their practice. Kai said that she knew this, but did the meditators know this, too?

Every morning, Zen practitioners chant the *Heart Sutra*, perhaps Buddhism's most famous sutra expounding the nature of reality. This chant is followed by a dedication that begins: "Buddha Nature pervades the whole universe existing right here, now." The dedication continues with "Whenever this devoted invocation is sent forth, it is perceived and subtly answered." How do you hear these words and experience their meaning? Your meditation itself pervades the whole universe. Everyone and everything are receiving and responding to it, whether they or you are aware of it or not.

The entire structure of the conditioned self, the so-called *me, mine, myself*, is called into question when we meditate. What is this so-called self? What are its limits? This gives rise to the fundamental spiritual question: Who am I? Answering this question does not require psychological or philosophical investigations, though you may go there at first. A spiritual quest can be entered from any direction. Eventually, though, the basic questions of spiritual life are resolved through one's own direct experiences.

And in direct experience, there is no boundary, no boundary at all.

Kai got a hug at night—breathing in her mother's meditation, breathing out her mother's meditation; breathing in everyone's meditation, breathing out everyone's meditation; breathing in the whole universe, breathing out the whole universe. Though you may think that you are limited in some way, everything is flowing through this vessel that you are. Can you experience this?

———

How far does your meditation extend? Show me! If you are not your boundary, then who are you? At the same time, how healthy are your boundaries?

MARTINA:
Horrible Monster

There are Buddhas and there are sentient beings.
Is there a difference?
There are monsters and there are sentient beings.
Is there a difference?

KOAN

Who is this horrible monster yelling at me?

REFLECTION

As enlightened mothers and fathers well know, kids can be monsters. In fact, with all its brilliant animators and technical wizardry, Hollywood hasn't come close to creating the monsters our own children can be. Nobody pushes our buttons harder, no one angers or pains us more, and no one drives us crazier.

Shakyamuni Buddha is often depicted as sitting with a serene smile on his face. The Jewish side of me tends to be suspicious of people who smile all the time. But the Buddha said that life is suffering. If I have two young children and both scream to be picked up, I can only pick up one with my two arms. So one child will be held and comforted, the other will probably scream even harder and later accrue lots of therapy bills.

Do I smile? Do I maintain equanimity?

Many of us want to find the secret to the Buddha's smile so that we can face any situation and stress with peace and calm. Often the situations are right in our homes. If we don't smile, if we lose our composure, we feel like Buddhist failures.

Historians tell us that Shakyamuni didn't wish any statues made of him, and indeed, for the first couple of centuries after his death none were made. Only much later did artisans start making statues of the Buddha, and as often happens, they built these likenesses in their image of him, or in their imaginings of what they and we would like to be—people who are serene at every moment.

Is that possible? We usually have two arms and two legs, not enough to take care of the entire universe, sometimes not enough to soothe even one child if you're tired. At times, doesn't your entire life seem to collapse into a monster's relentless cry?

You can react with anger, frustration, and blame, especially self-blame. Instead, can you let those go and bear quiet witness to your joint humanity—the crying of the monster, his funny Donald Duck baseball cap, your own tired body aching for sleep, the sun shining happily, the water boiling in the kettle, all the different lives and needs pushing up against each other, intersecting in a seemingly disorderly and even violent way?

On a dime, beasts can turn into beauties. The reverse is true as well. What do you do in the face of such change? What do you do with such a fast succession of emotions—from affection to anger to pouting to love and kisses to rage and indignation—all in a short space of time?

Many meditators have altars in a quiet room or corner of their home. Sometimes there's a small Buddha statue on the altar, sometimes there are flowers, candles, stones, or incense sticks. When there's turmoil and upset, they like to sit in front of the altar, if only for a few minutes, take deep breaths, gather back their energies, and bring them home.

But you can't always be near your altar when things fall apart, so what do you do? You might pay attention to your breath, the floor under your feet, the earth holding everything up, including you and the Buddha that has turned into a monster. In fact, the room surrounding that little monster itself becomes an altar with things arrayed in front: a teddy bear on the bed, the Buddha's dirty T-shirt on the floor, a cellphone attached to the Buddha's ear.

When you do that, doesn't something begin to beat strongly and steadily inside? There is no one to protect or react to because that beat includes the monster, you, and everything in the universe. Listening to it, you can determine what to do. Maybe you speak softly and soothingly to the monster; maybe you prepare his favorite food, watch her favorite television program with her, take him to the mall.

And maybe you leave the monster alone. A student related that she took her daughter to the dentist. These appointments always caused terrible upsets for her child and on the way home her daughter yelled and screamed the entire way. A few miles short of home, the mother stopped the car and got out by a small park. Sitting on a large rock, she paid attention to her breath, watched the birds, and felt the warm sun on her back. When the hollering stopped in her car, she got back in and drove them both home.

Challenging, monstrous times invite us to find our way home. What home is that? Maybe it is our basic humanity. Some people refer to it as Buddha Nature and others as basic goodness. Be it an angry child, a mean-spirited boss, or an event that shakes you to the very core—abide there and be fully present.

The more we practice this, the less repellent or frightening the monster becomes. Our limits and sensibilities, curbing our willingness to embrace life as it is, become more fluid, allowing us to function more freely even in the middle of a maelstrom. Over time an immense capacity arises—not just for the yelling of one horrible monster, but also for the cries of many monsters, in fact for the cries of the world.

Where will you go for refuge when the monster in your life starts yelling at you?

Liz's Blindness

I'll see it when I believe it.

KOAN

Liz has been blind all of her life and has never seen the face of her daughter. One day she took a photo with her iPhone, showed it to her sighted daughter and asked, "How does it look?"

Her daughter replied, "Mom, it looks like it was taken by a blind person."

Liz replied, "No!"

REFLECTION

There are many different ways of seeing, not just through our eyes. Liz once tried to teach a young man how to walk without the use of his eyes. He was in the upstairs hallway of her house for the first time and she blindfolded him. Soon he realized that if he really paid attention, he could sense the walls of the hallway. It almost felt like they were reaching out to him, he told Liz. He started walking and didn't bump into anything.

We depend so much on our six senses in order to experience life; for this reason, Liz is often technically described as *visually impaired*. But aren't we "seeing" folks impaired because we cling so much to seeing in order to experience things? Our eyes—and our other senses, too—are blind to many aspects of life. If you don't believe that, watch the tips of your dog's ears flip sideways as they catch sounds you can't catch. Watch his nostrils, containing three hundred million olfactory receptors (as opposed to our six million), quiver with excitement as they process scent-based information that is not available to us humans.

Dajian Huineng, the Sixth Chinese Patriarch, became enlightened from hearing one line from the *Diamond Sutra*: "Abiding nowhere, raise the Mind." To arouse it, we can't be attached to the forms and appearances our eyes reveal, the sounds we hear through our ears, or the smells we get through our nose. Not only can't our senses access all of life, they also contain filters that sift through all the material constantly streaming in and send only a fraction of it to the brain, which then does its own winnowing based on criteria too numerous to mention, before we begin to be aware of anything.

Like everything else, what we see, hear, smell, touch, taste, and think arises, then passes. Does any of it have a permanent reality of its own? Nevertheless, don't we mercilessly try to manipulate and control our lives, as well as other people's lives, according to this very limited evidence of our senses?

Some traditions and cultures have stories of miracles that great men and women perform: levitation, bringing the dead back to life, the parting of waters, the appearance of spirits and angels. The miracle we have in Zen is letting go. It's the practice of not attaching to anything, realizing that what we see, hear, smell, touch, and taste is highly conditioned and constantly changing, with nothing definitive and substantial of its own. It's when we hold on lightly, being curious rather than critical, that something new opens up.

Jacques Lusseyran became completely blind after an accident at the age of eight and wrote that it was only then that he saw light everywhere,[17] light that seeing people were blind to. He became a leader of young French Resistance fighters during World War II and was able to maneuver his way through Nazi-occupied Paris, relying on instinct, intuition, and a quality of vision that eluded others.

From the sublime to the mundane: My husband was color-blind. He'd come out of our bedroom wearing a combination of colors that made me laugh: brown slacks, green shirt, and a purple sweater, or a burgundy T-shirt with khaki safari pants. He'd grin and shrug: "They match, right?" Sometimes we went back and picked out different things for him to wear, and sometimes we didn't. Either way, my sense of *match* got a whole lot bigger thanks to his color blindness.

When you can't see, everything matches perfectly.

What do you see when you can't see? What do you hear when you can't hear? When cataracts take away your vision, are you any less whole than you were before?

ESTHER:

Me, My Daughter, and Five Men

Men, women, sons, daughters, brothers, sisters—
Tell me, to whom belongs the Dharma?
If you say that True Self is neither man nor woman,
What will you do on your honeymoon night?

KOAN

Esther and her daughter were two females living with five males: Esther's husband and four sons. Esther asked: *How can I hear my daughter's voice among five men?*

REFLECTION

Sometimes people write that gender has no place in Zen, that it's an artificial construct in a practice that urges us to realize our lack of an individual, separate self. If there is no such thing as a separate self, what is this thing called *man* and *woman*, *male* and *female*?

I am not a separate self, and at the same time I am different. So how do you honor the individual voice of each member of the family? How do you listen to the soft and the loud, the shy and the bold, the quiet and the noisy? How do you respect the different personalities of boys and girls without falling into stereotypes, without dictating preferences?

Don't we all have our personal preferences? Our society has preferences, too: for the prosperous over the poor, white people over those of color, the young over the aged, men over women. All are equal in their differences. Intuitively, we think that our equality lies in our oneness, but it actually lies in our differences, in the sense that no single "difference" is bigger, more important, or of higher value than any other difference—except according to someone's preference.

Is it easy to raise a daughter in our society? Is it easy to read that millions of female fetuses have been aborted in Asia and millions of girls everywhere left illiterate, uneducated, unfed, and uncared for because they're girls? My mother remembered that in her large, poor family in Eastern Europe, the girls helped their mother prepare the food and then watched as the boys came in and ate; they didn't eat until the boys finished, and then they only ate what was left. For many years, she disliked women, calling them weak and spineless, and she preferred the company of men. She wished to be one of the strong ones, the loud ones, the ones who could eat first.

How do you hear your daughter's voice without succumbing to stereotypes, without expecting her voice to be softer than her brothers', more tentative and submissive? Could she be as loud as they are, as rambunctious and assertive? How long will it take before someone—at home, in school, or a neighbor or friend— finally tells her that girls don't behave that way?

Freedom comes out of realizing that every single thing has its place and position, that each and every person and thing is the One Body—men, women, young, old, black, white, plants, animals, sentient and insentient beings. For this reason, isn't our practice to let go of all labels and return again and again to the question: Who am I? Answers come up right away: a woman, a teacher, a writer, the one making dinner, the one walking the dog, a daughter speaking to her mother by phone. But all these things can change, so who are you really?

The practice is to dwell in that question rather than in the label.

Once you see that the One Body expresses itself equally in all the different forms of life, doesn't honoring one form over another miss the point? If that One Body includes everything without exception, how can you question the value of, or denigrate, any of its expressions?

Nevertheless, it has taken years to uncover the names of female Buddhist nuns and teachers who have taught this precious dharma since the time of Shakyamuni. The names of male teachers have been chanted from the beginning, but only recently have some of us added the names of female teachers as well. Most of the names of women teachers have disappeared into the dust of history, and for this reason, in dedicating our prayers and chants to them, we invoke *all Women Honored Ones whose names have been forgotten or left unsaid.*

Awareness of how others discriminate or look down on us due to our gender, color, or religion helps us respond appropriately. But getting resentful and self-righteous shows my attachment to the label. It will provide a temporary answer to the question of who I am, but it will not help me sit in the space of not-knowing.

Does your true nature have anything to do with labels or descriptions?

My husband had a major stroke that paralyzed half his body. He was quite disabled even after two years of therapy and exercise, and a bout with cancer did not help. People called him a stroke victim, or a stroke survivor, but is that what he was?

Once we were being interviewed for a film on Zen and peacemaking. He stared straight at the interviewer with two patches on his nose and forehead from the cancer surgery and radiation, half his face swollen and black and blue from a bad fall he'd had the previous night, and stitches at his temple fastening a deep, painful cut. He was worn and tired that day, his eyes dimmer than before but still containing his old spark, and he spoke slowly, with effort:

"We had in our house a big glass vase. One day it broke into many pieces. Tell me, was it whole then, and is it now broken? It was whole when it was in one piece, and it's whole when it's in many pieces. In fact, each small fragment is the whole." He thought for a minute, then continued: "Two years ago I had a big stroke. Anyone seeing me before my stroke would have said that I was whole. Now, two years after the stroke, and with cancer, tell me, am I any less whole?"

Whole—and different. All of us are equal and different manifestations of this one great life. When I'm aware of this, can I "listen" to the butterfly as deeply as I listen to another human being? Can I bear witness to the sharp quills of porcupines, the slither of snakes, the large, smelly turd piles left by horses? Can I bear witness equally to boys and girls, women and men, honoring each for his and her difference, his and her uniqueness?

———

Look carefully at anything: a pen, a tree, a bottle of water, your child. Describe it in your mind. Now look again and let go of the words and labels you came up with earlier. Tell me, what remains?

WALTER:
No Labels

I am the concerned parent.
I am the intolerant family.
I am the disowned teenager.
I am the one who loves who I love.
Tell me, what are your true names?

KOAN

Walter's teenage daughter was a lesbian. When his daughter's girlfriend was tossed out of her home by her parents, Walter and his wife took her in until they could locate another family member for her to live with. It was a complex time when both families had to face many truths about their daughters and themselves.

After the girlfriend had been safely relocated, Walter and his wife said to their daughter, "You have our full support and love as a lesbian."

Their daughter replied, "I don't need labels. I love who I love."

Walter realized the limitations of his views.

REFLECTION

Call me whatever you wish, it is not me.

Labels have their uses and applications, but present a conundrum for those seeking to see beyond labels into the essence of things. When you affix a label to someone, such as *lesbian*, *Asian*, or *fat*, the image of the person becomes static, fixed in your mind as a concept or idea rather than the fully alive, ever-changing person before you. Concepts about a person block you from seeing and experiencing the depth and uniqueness of the person himself.

The same is also true when you apply a name or label to yourself. For many years, I was called Wendy. After I received my spiritual name, I was called Egyoku. After many years as Egyoku, I asked myself, "Whatever happened to Wendy? Where did she go?" So I brought Wendy and Egyoku together. I myself had become identified with these names in different ways. Regardless of whom those names represent, the fact is that I am *like this*.

Who are you? This brings us back to the same fundamental question: Who am I?

Walter's teenage daughter knew that she was not a label. She knew that *lesbian* meant different things to different people and to society as well, and she could not locate herself in these meanings. I recall a story told by Chan Master Sheng Yen, who was leading a retreat and recognized that one of the students was close to a breakthrough. So he asked the student, "What is your name?" The student replied, "Ch'en." Master Sheng Yen said, "That's wrong. Ch'en is over there!" and he pointed to the name card

93

pasted on the wall above his cushion. Ch'en said, "What am I doing over there?" Ch'en was lost in his name.[18]

Do you so identify with your name that you think that's who you are? Do you identify someone else with an idea that prevents you from seeing the totality of that person?

Walter was surprised when his teenage daughter fell in love with another girl, but he supported her choice. The family of his daughter's girlfriend, adamantly opposed, tossed her out and she sought refuge in Walter's home. Since she was a minor, Walter and his wife worked to find a relative of the girlfriend to take her in. When all was finally settled, the two parents spoke to their daughter, acknowledged her choice, and expressed their unequivocal support.

"I don't need labels," their daughter replied.

She revealed a marvelous wisdom: *I am not a label. I am not your idea of a lesbian. I am not even my idea of a lesbian. I am not your idea of "my teenage daughter"; in fact, I am not your idea of anything.* What do you do when presented with such a powerful teaching?

Walter immediately understood what constraints he'd imposed both on his daughter and on himself. His teenage daughter became a teacher for him. He vowed to set aside his ideas about who she was and wasn't, and willingly opened himself to meeting anew the being before him. He acknowledged his need to protect her, and at the same time realized that his deep love for her was best expressed by dropping his ideas about who she was.

"I love who I love," she said.

The history of humankind up to today overflows with stories of those who loved who they loved and were punished for it. Humans have forever tried to manipulate, control, and render love predictable. In fact, *love* is perhaps the biggest label of all.

Imagine someone you know. How do you see this person beyond the names and labels you give him or her? The Sufi poet Rumi said, "Out beyond ideas of wrongdoing and rightdoing there is a field. I will meet you there." Meet the person you are imagining—a co-worker, a beloved, a housemate—in the place beyond knowing and beyond not-knowing. Where is this place? Who do you see?

———

Tell me, what are your true names?

DEB:
Colic

The seagull doesn't know it's flying south in autumn;
The fox stalking a squirrel in the snow doesn't even know
    it's hungry.
If they don't know what they're doing, how can they do
    so much?

KOAN

The student approached the teacher urgently. "My baby has had colic for five days!"

"My baby once had colic for ten days," the teacher said.

"I don't know what to do," moaned the student.

"I found out exactly what to do," said the teacher.

"Quick!" the student begged. "Tell me what you did!"

"I asked the Master," the teacher replied.

REFLECTION

Who's the Master?

Isn't it interesting how often we want someone or something to be in charge and tell us what to do? How often we distrust the unfolding of our own life and place more confidence in other people's experiences? And if it's not a person we turn to for answers, it's something else: We toss the I-Ching, buy the latest self-help book, and even return again and again to a set of principles or a body of knowledge we've used in the past (*It's worked until now!*).

Sometimes we take refuge in our brain: *I'll think about it, I'll analyze it, I'll figure it out*. But as the Catholic contemplative Richard Rohr said: "We don't think ourselves into a new way of living. We live ourselves into a new way of thinking."[19] Being right here moment by moment, with no preconceived notions from the past or expectations of the future, this most intimate way of being, is what tells us what to do.

But we want to get it right, right? All we have to do is find the right text, model, teaching, or YouTube video, and we'll know how to do life. Or at least kids.

Bearing witness, on the other hand, can be full of trial and error, of trying this and that, of meandering efforts that often don't give us the result we wished for but something else entirely. Is there anything perfect about it?

Of course, it makes a lot of sense to ask for advice and help when raising any child; parents have done that from the beginning of time. But taking care of a baby with colic is a powerful practice in meeting the here-and-now with no resolution in sight. Most babies cry because they want something: food, drink, to be held, to go to sleep. A baby with colic cries for no apparent reason.

Changing or feeding the baby won't help; the distress is obvious and intense, but usually there's very little anyone can do to stop the crying. Our mind naturally scurries back and forth, trying to find something to do; we call our friends, our mothers, our doctors; we read books, we pray—and the baby keeps on crying.

Not-knowing does not mean *I don't know what to do*. Isn't the *I* still there? Listen to it: *But I should know what to do, I'm not a good mother, I'm exhausted after five nights of no sleep, I hate myself, I wish this would end!* Not-knowing is about letting go of answers and resolution, and unconditionally opening to the moment.

Right now, that means opening up to a wailing baby who may keep on wailing for a long time. When there's nothing to do, what do you do?

Throughout your life, haven't you found yourself in situations where you're at a loss, where your hard-working efforts don't show up in the results? A good friend talked about raising a son with mental illness. She and her husband tried different kinds of schools and different doctors and therapists, read every book and article, talked to other parents and friends, did everything they could think of, and often felt like they'd hit a wall, that nothing they did made much difference. Those were dark and clear times both, she said. She saw how life could unfold regardless of her deepest wishes and fears, beyond her capacities and understanding—an unfathomable life. It took many years, but finally, rather than feeling lost or bewildered, she found there a measure of peace and even confidence.

Can you remember to breathe as you hold the baby? Can you feel the warmth of the baby's clothes? Can you still smell the baby's sweet skin? Can you notice how anxious you are about your mothering? How you want certain moments to end or be different from what they are? How you want to fix things?

Slowly you let go of all that and bear simple witness: to the baby's wail, your nervous fear and exhaustion, and also, perhaps, the deep stirrings of love and compassion that arise even when— or especially when—you don't know what to do.

———

What do you do when you feel powerless? How does it feel in your body? Can you hear the accusations and reproaches in your mind? Can you let go and bear witness?

———— ————

BARBARA:
What Is Best?

———— ————

—*I'm leaving home.*
—*I beat him up because he called me names.*
—*I'm too fat so I've stopped eating.*
—*I want to drop out of school and smoke dope.*

If you know what to do, you fall.
If you can't decide, you fall too.
If you lie awake at night staring up at the ceiling, how
    does that help?

KOAN

As a mother, Barbara often had to make decisions for her children: When would they be ready for kindergarten? Which school would be best for them? How late could they stay out as teenagers? One often behaved differently from the others: resisted going to kindergarten, made too much noise in school, was too quiet, etc. Often teachers, family, and friends had clear opinions about what to do, while Barbara and her husband felt they did not know.

She had the same koan for many, many years: What is best for you, my child?

REFLECTION

How many sleepless nights do you suffer when your child doesn't follow the rules? How many arguments do you have with your husband or wife about your children? How many concerned discussions do you have with teachers and counselors? How many exhortations, appeals to common sense, and promises of sticks or carrots do you make until you finally collapse on a chair in exhaustion, stare into outer space, and wonder if there's anything harder than being a parent?

Aren't we supposed to be a little more detached? Many people think that's what Buddhism is all about: some way of making things clean, calm, and clear. But does clarity emerge from seeking an optimal, perfect solution, or from letting go of the delusion that such a thing exists?

Returning to a state of not-knowing calls you to let go of self-centered habits and concerns, such as: *Am I a good enough mother? Am I too strict or too loose? Why doesn't he do what I tell him?*

We can become tense, anxious, and angry, or we can make things more workable. We look deeply at our ingrained habits and tightly held beliefs, such as always having a clean house, always serving a healthy meal, always being available, perfect, and in control. Letting go, we open up the hand that clutches at idealizations of the perfect child and the perfect parent.

Even less helpful are the comparisons: *He is not like the others, she is in the bottom fortieth percentile, he doesn't participate enough, she has ADHD*, etc. Data-based generalizations may have some value, but often have nothing to do with the uniqueness of your child. *She isn't like the other kids on the block.* Not only isn't she like the others, she's not even the way she was a minute ago. Can you bear witness to her individuality and ask how she could bloom into the fullness of herself? How he or she can become exactly who he or she is?

How closely attuned are you to the unique and distinct aspects of your child? To develop such attunement, you may have to let go of others' comparisons and advice. Is there a personal agenda you're trying to implement here? An ambition or vision of your own that you wish to actualize? Can you step back from all of that and ask: What is best for you at this moment? When the answer arrives, hold it lightly and ask the same question the next day, opening to a new answer again and again.

Judging, comparing, measuring, testing, and evaluating have their uses. But when they take all the oxygen in the room and shrink-wrap life into a statistical formula, we lose vision and confidence in our child and ourselves. Letting go of that delusion of expertise and perfect knowledge is not just a great relief, but also helps us return to not-knowing.

Sit for five minutes and breathe. Your life is challenging, and at the same time workable. Your child's life, too, is workable. Bear close witness to its fluidity, its individuality, its unexpected twists and turns. Instead of trying to make it perfect, just ask over and over the question: Who are you, my child? What is best for you?

———

When you let go of certainty and perfection, what's left? How do you feel when you tell yourself that you don't know what to do? Can you smile when you say that?

JUDITH:
Vigil

In the end, after many years,
She sets out across the sea.
I keep a lookout on the beach
Though nothing much happens.

KOAN

It's so late at night; why isn't she home yet? I am trying to squash the panicking thoughts and rising nausea. Is it sex? Is it drugs? Has she been knocked off her bike and taken to the hospital? Has she been abducted for the sex trade in the East, never to be heard from again? This is hell!

Why isn't she home yet?

REFLECTION

It is 2:00 in the morning, 3:00, 4:00, 5:00. The sun begins to rise. It's now 6:00 in the morning and she's still not here.

Is there anything left to do? You've done everything you could to protect your children, fed and sheltered them, prepared them for the world. And all it takes is one night when they're late coming home to make you realize that it's not enough, that it never will be enough. In this case, even when the daughter is grown up and in a performing arts profession that calls for her to be up into the early hours most nights, the old gnawing fear is still there: *She's not home yet.*

These are the times, people say, when they feel special gratitude for their meditation practice, the times when the world feels like a horror film, monsters lying in ambush and catastrophe just around the corner. Some years ago, a new mother told me that night after night she had nightmares about what could happen to her son: He'll crash in an airplane, he'll drown in the ocean, he'll be in a train that will derail. "You wouldn't guess he's only two," sighed her husband.

When your children were in your belly it felt as though everything depended on you. Once the umbilical cord is cut, babies' wellbeing also depends on other people, including strangers. As they grow up, the world opens to receive them, they leave home and go far away; from day to day, you are less able to protect them, till finally you must leave them completely.

That's in the best of situations. Sometimes parents lose children at an early age. One woman lost her daughter in a road accident just as the young woman was entering a new career and enjoying a loving relationship. Over the course of several years she retraced her daughter's footsteps, going to places her daughter had visited, feeling, she said, like the goddess Demeter searching for her daughter Persephone in the underworld. But even the goddess could only save her daughter from Hades for six months each year before her daughter returned to the Land of the Dead.

Those kinds of tragedies are hard enough, but how do we practice for even a natural course of events that will lead to a parting of the ways with our children? Can you practice this evening, when she's not home on time or when he doesn't answer his phone? Whenever anxiety manifests—a sinking feeling in the belly, constriction in the lungs, and voices in the mind that yell doom— go back to basics and turn your attention to the breath. Plunging into inhalation and exhalation brings you into contact with the natural rhythms of life and the essence of all things, which is space, vast enough to contain even the stormiest of minds. When you breathe deeply, you experience yourself as that vast space, with life inhaling and exhaling through you.

A line in the Heart Sutra says: "Thus Bodhisattvas live this Prajna Paramita with no hindrance of mind. No hindrance, therefore no fear." Hindrances of mind arise from attachment. Who do you feel more attached to than your children? Isn't it the most powerful tie there is? In both subtle and gross ways, a loving state of mind can congeal with resentment and curdle into obsessiveness and fear. That's when even the greatest love in the world becomes a prison, both for the person we love and for ourselves.

Is this the natural outcome of love? How do I experience life as it is, boundless and ungraspable, with no fear? Fear extends out into the future, evoking frightening scenarios of what can happen in the next moment, the next hour, the next day. You can let go of such scenarios by returning to this moment, to this breath, to this human being right now.

And sometimes we can't do it. When the same nightmares come back again and again, no matter how hard we try, it may be best to do something else entirely. Create a ceremony, speak your wishes out loud, use your voice rather than keeping silent: *May my child be safe*. Light an incense stick, prostrate yourself on the ground, engage your entire body.

In Zen, we treat the body-mind as one entity. Moving your body creates more fluidity in the mind; walking in the woods improves the function and connectivity of brain cells. Some people clean their house from top to bottom when they're anxious. As they plunge into dusting, washing, and vacuuming, their mind clears. Or else they garden, turning over the soil or weeding attentively.

Life's arc is beyond our understanding, but when I take refuge in this moment, I experience deep intelligence at work everywhere. If all we can hear is the voice of fear and despair inside, we remain captive to a small, constricted, self-centered version of life; when we remember and practice the breath of the universe, the windows open wide onto a limitless horizon.

———

Can you "sit" with your fear? If not, can you walk with it, clean your house with it, play out the fear on a musical instrument? When you feel the universe rapidly shrinking around you, where do you find your breathing space?

JINEN:
Daniel's Teeth

Cracks aren't what they're cracked up to be.

KOAN

Jinen's son, Daniel, has grown up with disabilities. As a result, though he is still a young man, his body has begun to deteriorate. Since he does not brush his teeth, they break and fall out. Jinen makes suggestions, but Daniel won't follow them. There have been many painful times like these over numerous years.

Daniel's teeth continue to decay and break. But tell me, has there ever been a crack?

REFLECTION

What fantasies and wishes do you have for your children? A good education, health, love, a family of their own, a life of their own? Some of what you hope for will happen, some won't. Some children can't hold onto jobs, some can't hold onto their health. Some never get married or have children, some never leave home. Some have poor personal hygiene resulting in teeth that yellow and fall out, and a body that breaks down at a young age.

Ernest Hemingway wrote: "The world breaks every one and afterward many are strong at the broken places."[20] Things crack all the time—not just teeth, but relationships, careers, families, health, holidays together. At the same time, there's a promise: *Many are strong in the broken places.*

What does it mean to be broken? What does it mean to be cracked? Don't we all have cracks somewhere—in our teeth, in our mind, in our life? You might say that Daniel's cracks are normal for him. You can go further and say that Daniel's cracks are his jewels.

I have a terrible fear of thunderstorms. The minute lightning used to strike near the house, my husband would give me an alert, discerning look. In recognizing my rising anxiety, he was also recognizing my cracks, the unique mix of qualities he thought of as his wife. Zen Peacemakers says its work takes place in the cracks, those places we try to skip over, ignore, or stay away from.

Sunflowers grow in the cracks, and so do we.

The areas of deepest pain, often connected to our children, are precisely the ones where we must pay deepest attention. The gap between life as it is and life as we'd like it to be is hardest here, the universe unfolding according to its own karmic laws as opposed to our fondest wishes. In that gap there's a sense of rawness, as though blinders have fallen off our eyes. Ideas, plans, assumptions, and dreams of the future—all have fallen by the wayside, into the cracks. In working with her son's cracks, Jinen's cracks appear as well, a ripe field of practice.

For hundreds of years, Chinese and Japanese Zen teachers would hit or yell at their students in an effort to catch them by surprise and break through the conceptual, self-centered veil that is part of our costume as humans. What were they trying to do if not to crack us wide open? Life with children can do that to us, too. And even as we grieve and mourn for a lost sense of normalcy (which is usually a synonym for how we think things should be), we could learn to appreciate these wide-open cracks that demand our attention and creativity, demand that we improvise moment by moment.

The refuge we call *this very moment* is the place where we experience the unity of all life, including youth, sunlight, spring, cancer, gauntness, and a mouth with no teeth. It includes Daniel and his mother's deep love for him, along with her frustration, upset, and disappointment.

How do you bear witness to such fullness? Not by denying heartbreak, but by being present. Bear witness, feel your child's hurt, hear his stubborn rejoinders, see both the smile and the rejection. Don't shut yourself off from anything. Can you see that even as your child is sick the birds still fly to the feeders; the sun shines, followed by a caravan of clouds, and then shines again; cars hurry to their destinations; and couples fall in love and kiss on park benches?

What is a "normal" life for you or your children? When life changes, is there a new "normal?" What happens to it?

WORK

ANDREA:
Nothing

Doing nothing is the great work.
Doing something is no big deal at all.

KOAN

Andrea wanted to do some work to benefit refugees in the German city in which she lived. She didn't receive much support, but had a deep conviction that this was the right moment and the right place for her to start—only what? Listening deeply and carefully, she heard her heart say: *Mach´ was draus! Make something of it.*

She now teaches German as a foreign language to refugees from all over the world in the city of Würzburg, where she lives.

She says she learned this: *Da ist nichts—mach´ was draus!* *There is nothing—make something of it!*

REFLECTION

Isn't there a difference between getting up in the morning knowing exactly what to do, and waking up to face a wide-open day: no schedules, no appointments, no requirements? That's when we realize how much we identify with what we do: a busy manager, a mother of four children, an IT consultant, a college teacher, an artist. For many of us, who we are is what we do, isn't it? As much as we complain about the busyness of our lives, it gives us a sense of stability and belonging; it gives us the plan.

But it's the not-knowing that is infinitely more interesting, the home of creativity, magic, and potential. If there is one thing on our day's schedule, we often fixate on it in the same way that we fixate on the one dot on a blank page. Our eyes are automatically drawn to the dot and we miss the bigger space around it. But when there is no-thing, there can be everything.

We say that the reason we do anything—write a book, help refugees, build a house—is because we want to do it. But isn't the reason we do something as Andrea put it: *There is nothing— make something of it?* The nothing manifests as something all the time, according to karmic conditions.

Xuefeng, a ninth-century Chan master, said: "If you set up a single atom of dust, the nation flourishes; if you do not set up a single atom of dust, the nation perishes."[21] Taking the initiative, creating or building anything, sets up a chain of events over which you have very little control. Good things happen, bad things happen. If you do nothing, then neither those good things nor those bad things will happen, but is that really what life is about?

Some of the most exciting things in my life have happened when I suddenly said I would do something with no forethought.

This book came into being when I was in the zendo listening to people describe home situations that plunged them into not-knowing, and without a thought I said aloud, "Let's put together a book on householder koans."

Bernie Glassman founded the Greyston Mandala to serve a poor area of southwest Yonkers in New York. One evening, at the height of the AIDS epidemic, he attended a presentation on HIV. Upon hearing that in the entire city of Yonkers there was no housing at all for people with HIV, he said without thinking: "Greyston will do it." When his own board of directors refused to take this on, he started a new organization to build that housing. Seven years and ten million dollars later, Greyston opened up the city's first apartments for people with HIV and a day center that was among the first in the nation to offer alternative therapies for people with AIDS.

Looking back on your own life, haven't you learned to trust that burst of spontaneity when you surprise yourself by saying, "I'll do that"? The response doesn't come out of plans or strategy, it seems to come out of nowhere, out of nothing.

"I would love to live like a river flows, carried by the surprise of its own unfolding," wrote the poet and philosopher John O'Donohue.[22]

Overwhelmed by the suffering in the world—racism, refugees, lack of medical care, climate change, vanishing species—many people say they don't begin to know where to start. There's a lot that needs doing, and like Andrea, they want to do something, only what? Are you one of them? Do you withdraw into some personal cave with a large television screen, feeling as though you've failed without even trying? "I want to do so much, and instead I'm drowning," one student said.

If you begin with not-knowing, you don't have to know anything ahead of time. Isn't that a relief? Choose any situation—needy children, families lacking nutritious food or adequate shelter, political change—and let go of your fixed ideas and opinions about them. You can tell how fixed they are and how attached you feel to them by the strong emotion of anger, resentment, or frustration that is often there. You know you've begun to let go when you experience more calm and confidence inside.

Now watch and listen deeply. What to do begins to emerge by itself. Maybe it's a creative, big idea. Maybe it's organizing and coordinating services among different groups. Maybe it's going back to school to acquire more skills and knowledge. And maybe it's something small, targeted, and doable, which works well with other aspects of your life.

Instead of staying in your head, get out there. Drive undocumented workers to their work, play with their kids in the daycare centers. Your strong desire to fulfill your Bodhisattva vows makes for very fertile ground, don't underestimate it. Set up that single atom of dust. It's a creative time, don't stifle it with too much thinking and figuring out. Do something small that's right in front of you. Get your body-mind moving. This will generate energy and momentum, putting you in the world of action rather than in perplexity and inaction.

You don't have to know anything ahead of time. Bearing witness will tell you what to do. Trust it.

Is the planet overwhelmed, or is your mind? If it's either, neither, or both, always go back to basics.

MYOKI:
Opening

Mickey, Minnie, Popeye, and Donald Duck:
Red shorts, white gloves, yellow shoes—
Don't they always talk the same?
Oh, boy! That sure is swell! Aw, gee!

KOAN

Myoki was giving a lecture to her fifth-grade class. Too many snow days meant she had to hurry to finish her curriculum. The students weren't happy about this. Suddenly, out of the corner of her eye, Myoki saw her pupil, Steven, standing upright by his desk. He'd gotten hold of her black sweater and was wearing it down over his thighs, like a short dress. Hands clasped against the side of his cheek, lips pursed, striking an enticing Minnie Mouse pose, he stared straight at her—all in the middle of class.

Myoki had an opening.

REFLECTION

The class held its breath as soon as I caught sight of Steven posing like that. Would I get angry? Would I reprimand him? What would I do?

Ahh, an interruption. Sudden, unexpected, confounding—and calling for a fast response.

You have work that you have to finish—a curriculum to follow, a book to write, a house to build, a child to get to school, a meal to cook, a computer to upgrade, flowers to plant—and you don't want any interruptions. But interruptions happen, so how do you react?

Gateless is the Great Tao
There are thousands of ways to it.[23]

Is there anything that is not a gate of practice? Every action you take, every situation you face, is an opportunity to experience yourself as whole. How? By plunging into the action or situation that presents itself. What happens when we call something an interruption? The implication is that we were doing something planned, maybe even important, and were unable to complete it because of the interruption. But the interruption is a gate, too.

Many years ago, I worked at the Greyston Bakery as part of the Zen Community of New York, which had its meditation room on the bakery's third floor. One Saturday, deep in meditation as part of a weekend retreat, I felt a hand on my shoulder. It was a baker asking me to come down because of a problem with a wedding cake due that day. Annoyed with this interruption, I followed him downstairs, and on the way to the finishing room picked up a piece of lemon cake that the bakers had left by the reception and put it in my mouth. The taste of lemon curd was a sudden shock. I came to a standstill, my senses reeling from a cake I had tasted many times before, and my mind opened in a way it had not two floors up, while doing meditation.

Albert Einstein proved years ago that time is an artificial construct, not real, but that doesn't prevent many of us from feeling stressed out due to time. Things happen *on time*, which means that they happen when we'd planned them to. On weekends and holidays, when we're relaxed, I feel that I have *lots of time on my hands*. On the other hand, if there are three hundred school days in a year and we lost many to weather, then my teaching may be *a race against time*.

Other cultures view time very differently. The Native American sense of time is more circular, connecting with the seasons, day and night, and the body's natural rhythms, all of which change continuously.

Have you ever rushed your children off somewhere, hurrying them to change their clothes, wash their face, and get into the car just when they're in the middle of some serious play, leaving them bewildered and angry? Do you feel out of sync with the natural, organic rhythms of life? Do you feel out of tune with the natural world, with sunlit days and dark nights, with seasons of life like youth and old age? We even try to manipulate the seasons through a contraption called Daylight Savings Time.

Interruptions may be life's way of reminding us that things are *time-less*, that changes are happening all the time that are not *timely*, that they have nothing to do with the concept of time, progress, or meeting goals and deadlines.

How mechanical is your life? Do you know what your body needs now? Is it food, rest, play? Do you eat because you're hungry or because it's time for dinner? Do you sleep because you're tired or because it's time to go to sleep? Is your practice paying attention to the needs and cadence of your body, and how these intersect with everything else in the universe, or is it looking at your watch, checking the time on your cell phone, avoiding anyone and anything that's not with the program, that's not *time-saving*?

Then Minnie Mouse stands up in your classroom and begs for your attention.

Do you go on as before, pretending you don't see her? Send Minnie to the principal's office? Tell her to sit down so that you could continue with what you were doing? Or is Minnie a gate into not-knowing? Bearing witness, what arises may be spontaneity, may be laughter.

If Minnie Mouse were to stand suddenly in front of you, what would you do?

JIMMIE:
Breakfast

"Ready to order?"
"I'll have the eggs enlightenment-side up, whole toast,
unconditioned orange juice, co-arising hash browns
and noncoffee."
"That'll be $7.49, please."

KOAN

A homeless man asks his friend, "Do you think we will ever work our way out of this?"

His friend replies, "Breakfast's at First Church today."

REFLECTION

Many of us did street retreats, living on the streets for a period of time with no money and just the clothes on our backs. We didn't pretend to be homeless, it was simply a time to explore life on the streets. Wherever we went, street people would tell us practical things: Where's the nearest soup kitchen? Who serves the best breakfast? Where can you find an extra pair of shoes? Where can you sleep at night undisturbed by the police?

Then we'd come home and get overwhelmed by the news and technology, by the fear of violence and war. *Do you think we'll ever work our way out of this?* We'd catch up with events around the globe, but lose sight of what's right in front of our faces. *Breakfast's at First Church today.*

Worrying about living isn't living; living is living. Watching the latest earthquake tragedy on TV is watching TV; it's not taking the smallest concrete step to take care of those that were hurt. A discussion with friends over a glass of wine about what's wrong with our country is talking and drinking, it doesn't create any change.

Breakfast's at First Church today. Take care of yourself and do something. Getting lost in distraction, the inflammatory language of political leaders or the media, or vague despondency and guilt helps no one.

How do we cut through abstractions? Sometimes even our way of helping can become an abstraction. Many years ago, my husband and I drove through the streets of San Francisco. Stopping at a red light, I saw a man holding out a cup asking for money, so I rolled down my window and gave him a dollar bill. He said thank you and I asked him his name. His eyes popped open. "Lady," he said, "I've been standing on this corner for a long time, and you're the first person who asked me my name."

Ask a panhandler on the street what his is name and he becomes Bob or John or Spencer. Hang out with him long enough and he won't be just Bob or John or Spencer, but a specific human being with a specific life story.

The homeless, the mentally ill, the poor, the immigrants. Part of what our brain does is label things, making order. But doesn't adding the preposition *the* make an object of human beings, like *the* tables or *the* chairs?

As the old Buddha said, "A painting of a rice cake does not satisfy hunger."[24] Don't we lose our life when we get lost in abstraction, when we go into our heads rather than bear witness? Hungry children, drowning polar bears, pandemics, the sex trade, refugees—these are all aspects of reality turned into headlines blasted at us by media, making the world feel like one great House of Horrors. What's real and what's an amusement park ride?

The Israeli writer David Grossman, in talking about the death of his son in war, said: "[W]e are doomed to touch reality through an open wound."[25] In some way, isn't that true for many of us? The temptation is to close things up, pretend they're not there, find multiple ways of hiding. When we're ready to face an open social wound, without retreating into illusion or abstraction, we discover movement and life there, or as Grossman said: "[W]ithin the pain there is also breath, creation, doing good."

The homeless are not the homeless. Some are natural leaders and entrepreneurs, setting up homeless camps, getting food and help for their friends. Some will give you the shirt off their backs and some will steal your shoes if you take them off while sleeping. Aren't they as different from each other as you are from me? Even their commonality—not having a home—differs from person to person depending on their life circumstances.

Zen is chopping wood and carrying water. It's taking the next step, doing what's right in front of you. The Buddha is famous for the practicality of his teaching, which was always aimed at relieving the suffering of the people who came to him. When Brahmins tried to engage him on more abstract theological questions, he maintained silence because he felt they were distractions from more immediate needs and concerns.

When the crisis with Syrian refugees flooding into Europe exploded, Pope Francis suggested that each European church and parish take in one family, a modest and relatively doable proposal. "They're not numbers," he said.

Don't get lost in adding and subtracting, don't get paralyzed by your own mind's abstractions. Help take care of one family. Help take care of one human being.

———

Do you know the name of one single homeless person on your corner? The name of one person holding up a sign for money? Can you tell them how to get to the local shelter? Can you take them there?

Louise Collects Eggs

A hen clucks, an egg is laid—
Warm, oval-shaped, a muted color.
When a woman collects the precious egg
What words of love does she utter?

KOAN

Louise talks lovingly to her chickens while she collects their eggs. One day, she noticed that the workman who was repairing the windows on her house was watching her, wiping tears from his eyes.

Self-conscious about being watched, she offered him a cup of tea or coffee and then, somewhat reluctantly, the eggs. He nodded yes and wiped his eyes.

She went into her kitchen to get a drink for the man and a bowl for the eggs, and found her son wiping tears from his eyes.

She asked her son, "Why are you crying?"

He replied, "I heard the worker say that the way you talk to your chickens when you collect eggs reminds him of his mother who died recently. He and I have become brothers watching you talking to the chickens and collecting eggs."

Louise was deeply affected.

REFLECTION

That person over there, is he your brother? Is she your sister?

A traditional koan asks you to manifest as an older or younger brother or sister. Here we have a young boy claiming a stranger as a brother because they've both watched their mothers talk lovingly to chickens while collecting eggs.

What does it mean to say that someone is your brother or your sister?

Indigenous people say we are all related. They address everyone as relatives. In our Western culture, isolation and separation often dominate. Using the phrase *all my relations* shifts us from identifying as separate individuals to feeling the fundamental connection of, as my teacher Taizan Maezumi Roshi would say: "All beings all together." What if you were to live from this place of radical inclusion and connection? What if you were to feel that everyone is your brother or sister, or, as the Tibetan Buddhists say, everyone has been your mother?

We are all related encompasses the cosmos and the earth, plants and creatures, and human beings. The Buddha himself declared upon awakening, "I, the great earth, all beings, are all together awake!"[26] All are of the same life force, of the same substance, appearing as different forms, shapes, colors, and textures. All is one; one is all. You cannot be separate from the life force or any of its expressions—not from chickens, eggs, other people, or even the dead.

What is called forth when you begin from a baseline of intimate connection to all?

The chicken world has a beautiful magic of call-and-response. A hen and chick must begin pecking at the same time for the eggshell to break and for the chick to emerge. If the chick pecks and there is no response, or if the mother hen pecks before the chick is ready, the chick dies. Zen Master Dogen Zenji wrote, "Although the color of peach blossoms is beautiful, they do not bloom of themselves; they open with the help of the spring breeze."[27]

Your life, too, is a ceaseless flow of calling others forth and being called forth by others. Your most basic needs—the food you eat, the clothes you wear, and the shelter you live in—depend on others' efforts. Whenever my teacher said to us, "My life only happens because of your lives," I felt uncomfortable until I realized that this is actually so. My life as well happens because of your life and innumerable lives unknown to me. Even though you may not be aware of these people, are they not also your relatives?

Can you see how far your life extends? I recall once when my teacher spoke about the chants we do before a meal. As he chanted, "Buddha was born in Kapilavastu," he began to cry. There it was: the moment of visceral connection that permeates time, space, and all beings.

Louise talking to her chickens while collecting their eggs called forth the memory of the worker's mother who had died and awakened her son's connection to a stranger whom he then called his brother. The whole universe is calling and responding, relative to relative, in one unceasing flow.

Who is pecking at your shell to draw you forth? Who is calling forth your kindness, tenderness, and beauty? Tell me: This person, is he your brother? Is she your sister?

———

What unexpected thing is calling you and how are you responding? What are you calling forth from another person? Is there anyone that you would not include in "all my relations"?

JAMES:
Cooked Greens

Boiling water breaks down molecular bonds
Transforming kale, oranges, even duck.
Tell me, has anything really changed here?
If not, why is everyone screaming?

KOAN

When James was head cook for a retreat, he told the teacher he heard kale greens screaming from the boiling soup pot.

The teacher said, "You should speak to Seppo about this." Seppo was the head cook in a Chinese monastery twelve centuries ago.

"But Seppo is long dead," James replied.

"Can't you hear him screaming?" asked the teacher.

REFLECTION

Seppo was the head cook in Tokusan's monastery and finally abbot of his own large temple in ninth-century China. There are also many tales of him and his companion, Ganto, making pilgrimages to various temples, thrusting and parrying with teachers and each other to gain a clearer understanding of life and practice.

What tales of food will appear in a thousand years about Zen meditators in the twenty-first century? That fruits and vegetables of all kinds surrounded them, no matter what the season? That while most people sorted apples before buying them, squeezing some and flinging others carelessly away, others didn't bother going to stores, just opened up their computer, highlighted on the screen organic roses grown in Guatemala and pineapples grown in Hawaii, and an hour later received both by drone? That some people didn't cook at all? That many starved while much food was thrown away?

Our lives in the West can occasionally feel safe and even complacent. But life and death are everywhere, in every act, including the simple activity of making soup. A Chan master said: *If I hold onto one thread of my robe, in fact I hold the entire robe.*[28] Doesn't making a salad reveal the world? Look at the purple onion you are slicing, or a single leaf of spinach. Contemplate the labors and laborers that have brought it to your kitchen; the sun, rain, and earth; and the life and death of the living plants that gave you these vegetables.

Or else plunge into the slicing and cutting of the onion. See its purple cloak unwind to reveal dark sections and thinner, lighter layers. Can you be so fully present in this activity that the onion is no longer an onion and you are no longer you?

Native cultures have always known that finding, cultivating, hunting, and preparing food demonstrate the entire cycle of life, from beginning to end. Here and now, with our clean, plastic-wrapped supermarkets, our microwave ovens and food processors, it's easy to think we can keep our distance from life's raw circumstances and its essential cycles.

Do we have the fearlessness and resolve to sit in the boiling cauldron? Who's the cook? Who is screaming and weeping? If we, indeed, are everything, aren't we each and every ingredient in the dish that's simmering on the stove?

List all the ingredients you use to co-create the meal of your life. Is there one that isn't you? Here is only a partial list of everything that's gone into the soup pot:

Beans, seasoning, pan, cook, apron, napkin, diner, butcher, cow,
sun, rain, pesticide, farmer, tractor, birds, clouds, worms, salt,
minerals, tractor, potholder, spoon, tongue, bowl, knife, tomatoes,
fertilizer, table, chair, tablecloth, onions, olives, oil,
trees, fire, water pump, well,
scientist, knife, blender,
earth

and
on
and
on.

In our meal chant, we say: "This food will pervade everywhere." What happens to the food you eat? How does it pervade everywhere?

DAISHIN:

Leaving the House

Creepy witches, dark forests, howling wolves—
I warned you not to leave the house!
If you don't know where you're going
Chances are you'll end up somewhere else.

KOAN

When a patient aims towards self-destruction, Daishin, a psycho-therapist and a student of the Way, leaves the house, too. How is it that, even while following a person with a disturbed mind, he never leaves the path?

REFLECTION

When a person becomes a Zen monk, it's said that she or he is leaving home. In this koan, therapists or teachers, while following a trail of confusion and pain, are also asked to leave something behind.

In fact, don't we all have to leave something behind when we join someone on his or her journey? What do parents leave behind when they join their children's journey into adulthood and beyond? What do doctors, nurses, and therapists leave behind as they accompany their patients into the land of serious illness and even death? What do Zen teachers leave behind as they work with their students over many years of training?

I think that what we leave behind is the answer, the notion that due to our greater experience, education, training, and recognition, we have an answer they do not, a definitive solution to someone's suffering.

"But they're looking to me for a solution, for a way out," one therapist said. "They come to me because of my expertise."

Expertise is good and useful; so are talk therapy and medication. But the Buddha's First Noble Truth taught that life is suffering because we crave and cling to things that will always change and never stay the same, never stay how we wish them to be. Love will come and go, work will come and go, and finally life as well. No therapist can remove this eventuality from a patient's life, nor his or her own life.

Many years ago a resident of our Zen community committed suicide. He had been admitted on condition that he take his medications, but he did not and finally put an end to his life. A long-time Zen practitioner and psychiatrist said to me: "Over the years I have worked with many patients who talked of suicide. Most of them never do it; a few have. If you're going to work with people like that, you carry that uncertainty with you, day after day."

We can't guarantee our patients anything. Accepting that is very difficult. Can you bear witness not just to the patient's words and actions but also to your own reactions: the nervous clutching

133

in your belly, the dry mouth, the fatigue and frustration? Even when self-destruction is not an issue, there is a sense of following someone into a place with no order, rules, consistency, or control. How does that feel? Are you attuned to yourself or just the patient?

What happens when you go home and your wife and children need attention? Do you yell at them to leave you alone and sit down in front of the television set? Do you feel you need a drink?

Try emptying yourself between patients, letting go of the story of one journey as you prepare for another. Can you find that point of stillness where nothing needs to be fixed, repaired, or changed in any way? The light of attunement need not go out when the patient walks out the door, it can continue shining inwards, directing our attention to the source. Where is this place? Is it inside the therapist? Is it in the patient?

Bearing witness to a patient's harrowing experiences, giving full permission, providing the generous space where so much is allowed to find expression, is a great gift. But tell me, who is being witnessed here?

> *Guishan asked Daowu, "Where are you coming from?"*
> *Daowu said, "I've come from tending the sick."*
> *Guishan said, "How many people were sick?"*
> *Daowu said, "There were the sick and the not-sick."*
> *Guishan said, "Isn't the one not sick you, Ascetic Zhi?"*
> *Daowu said, "Being sick and not being sick have nothing to do with him at all."*[29]

Who is sick, and who is not sick? And who is *him*? Even in highly fraught situations, the wall separating health and illness, patient and clinician, is a permeable one. How fixed are you in your position as the healthy one, the one with certainty and answers? Some of us are visibly traumatized, some hardly show scars. But aren't we all vulnerable to the vicissitudes of life, not to mention our human legacy of illness, old age, and death? Right now, I'm the therapist listening to someone's trauma, but on my way home tonight I could be in an accident, suffer brain injury, and be unable to function independently. It can happen in a flash. On what side of the desk will I be sitting then?

This is not *I* the therapist helping *you* the patient or even saving you. At this moment, I may have the expertise you are looking for—but later, or under different circumstances?

I was once on a street retreat in New York City with someone who'd worked all his life with people with mental illness. He said he'd like to bring all his co-workers—therapists and social workers—onto the streets so that they could see the people they were treating differently. The people he medicated and counseled in his office became his teachers on the streets, telling him where to eat and sleep, how to take care of himself.

Our life is sickness and health together, leaning one way or the other depending on circumstances. Understanding this, whose journey is this? How close will you get? Who are you afraid for? And when diagnoses and prescriptions no longer hold, what abides?

You are the therapist, the doctor, the social worker, the teacher. Tell me, what must you leave behind?

DAIKAN:
Names

He-Who-Must-Not-Be-Named
Has a name, after all.
Say it!

KOAN

Daikan attended the weekly meeting of a social service agency where the staff argued about how to refer to the people being served. Some thought they should be called clients, others wanted them to be called program participants. Some didn't understand why they couldn't be called patients, which was an old, widely-used label. The program director finally asked them, "If *you* were being served by this program, what would you want to be called?"

REFLECTION

What do you want to be called?

Most people call me Eve. Back in the 1990s, I was mostly called Myonen, the dharma name I received in a precepts ceremony. My parents called me Chavale, an affectionate version of Chava, the Hebrew name I was given at birth.

Maybe you think that these are three different names for the same person, but is it the same person? Eve is my name as an adult, used by my friends. Chavale brings back not only family associations but also East European *shtetls*, the trauma of the Holocaust, and a religious Jewish upbringing. Myonen evokes Zen training, Japan, and the companionship of other Zen practitioners. I migrate from one world to another, depending on the name I'm called. Not only does my behavior change, but also my language. I am all the things evoked by these names.

My teacher had dharma names galore, but he preferred to use *Bernie* because of its associations with his Jewish communist roots. When you called him Bernie, his behavior, intonation, and slang evoked Brooklyn, New York, where he grew up. And he began to behave pretty outrageously if someone called him Boobysattva, the name he chose for himself when he founded the Order of Disorder, an order of clowns.

What's in a name? Family history, a parent's expectations, a lover's whisper. Remember the significance of nicknames in school? Now think of titles like *Ms.* vs. *Miss* vs. *Mrs.*, and descriptive labels like *patient* vs. *client* and *mentally retarded* vs. *mentally challenged*. Why do these generate strong passions and controversy? In fact, people are beaten and killed every day over names: *Honky! Nigger! Jew! Arab! Faggot! Loser! Infidel! Witch! Slut! Communist! Capitalist! Terrorist!*

Do names capture who we really are? Can words capture the totality of life? The best name in the world only points to something;

it is not the thing itself. So how do we remember that *moon* is not the moon? That *chocolate* doesn't begin to capture that impossibly dusky concoction? And what about the word *love*?

Some of us take shelter in silence. No confusion there, right? "I just want to sit quietly," someone says to me in the meditation hall. *I don't want to have to talk, I don't want to have to listen, I just want silence.* But silence can conceal and mislead, too, as can anything we use as an escape from life. Zen meditation is a silent but active engagement with whatever arises, not an invitation to withdraw into Peter Pan's Neverland.

Many years ago I sat with my teacher to plan the schedule for a one-day retreat that began at 6:00 a.m. and ended at 9:00 p.m. He inserted three liturgical services along with three ritualized meals, a talk, and a few hours of housework as well as gardening. Since most of the attendees were new, the day would also include an introduction to meditation along with training in meal set-up and service, and training for the liturgy.

"So when do we sit?" I quipped.

He got angry. "We eat three meals because folks have to eat. For this reason, we also cook, serve, and clean. We do three services a day, all of which require training. And since the retreat is taking place here in this house, the house needs care, too. A silent retreat doesn't mean that we don't take care of things."

Words are no escape; silence is no escape. Words and names are important, but please remember that while the person is fluid, the name is not. That's probably why people change their names.

We're constantly expressing ourselves, even if all we do is stay in bed. A stranger will learn a lot about us from just watching us drink a cup of tea. So how do we drink a cup of tea? How do I talk to my doctor, or to my child? What names do I call her?

———

What happens when you forget someone's name? How do you relate beyond words and letters? Is silence all that's left?

INZAN:
Red Traffic Light

Green-yellow-red-yellow-green-red-red-red-yellow
Go-slow-stop-slow-go-stop-stop-stop-slow—
Wait a minute, it's too much!
How do you expect me to get anywhere?

KOAN

What is Buddha?
   A red light.

REFLECTION

We are in a hurry to get somewhere and the traffic light turns red. We can get irate and mutter under our breath, watching carefully for that first sign of green in order to press the accelerator. Or we could pause. Take a deep breath. Feel our body on the seat. Maybe adjust the seat belt so that it doesn't pinch our shoulder. Maybe look out at our surroundings, remind ourselves that life is not just about getting somewhere by a certain time.

"When it's a green light, I just go," a young driver said. "When it's red, I get that life has other plans."

Look at the irritation that comes up when a light turns red just as I'm hurrying to get somewhere. There's a quick exhalation of annoyance and my lips become a thin, disapproving line, my shoulders stiffen, my body constricts, maybe I mutter four-letter words under my breath. The universe is thwarting me, and I go into fighting mode.

What is this old instinct to control our environment, control our life? Can you become aware of your resentment when it feels as though life is controlling *you* through a computerized traffic light? That sounds funny, until we remember how much hurt people inflict on themselves and others due to traffic, stalled highways, and blinking lights. Sometimes we turn our aggression on other motorists, the police, or pedestrians on the road, but always we turn our aggression on ourselves. If you don't believe that, look at your face in the rearview mirror next time you hit an unwanted red light.

One student said that she doesn't put the radio on when she drives for forty minutes to work. She has a family at home and students at school. "My driving time is just for me," she said. "When I drive, I just drive. When someone veers in front of me, I hit the brakes. When traffic slows down, I slow down. It's very simple, never complicated. Life tells me what to do, and I do it."

Do you like to complicate things?

An old koan tells of the Chan Master Deshan, first a scholar and translator, and then head of a large monastery. After years of teaching, getting old, he comes out one day holding his eating bowls.

Seeing him, a student monk berates him: "Don't you know the meal bell hasn't rung and the drum hasn't been struck yet?"[30] At which point the old teacher just turns around and returns to his room. He doesn't argue, he doesn't remind the student who's boss, he doesn't get defensive about being old. He doesn't complicate things.

We eat when the bell rings. We drive when the light turns green, and we stop when it turns red.

When we act in consonance with things as they are, doesn't everything open up? There's no longer just concern about coming to work on time, there's also an autumn sky, a woman in a pink jacket pushing a perambulator across the street, a truck delivering winter oil, a man opening up the shutters of his store, the car purring contentedly after its servicing the other day. I stop grasping at goals and destinations.

Bees carry pollen and nectar to feed their young, flying from flower to flower much like we drive from place to place. But as they fly they also drop pollen from one flower onto another, thus pollinating flowers and plants. They are doing their thing, and at the same time participating in a highly intelligent, complex life cycle. Humans hit the road in order to pick up children, go to work, buy food for our family. At the same time, life is happening not just around us but also through us.

On the Green River Zen Center website, we have *Regular Schedule* and *Special Events*. In life, we have our Regular Schedule too: breakfast, go to work, lunch, a doctor's appointment, pick up the kids from school, etc. And then there are Special Events: a car accident, a serious illness, a promotion, a birth, a death.

In the end, there's only Life's Schedule. Aren't you doing that retreat forever? Sometimes it's about moving forward, sometimes it's about turning right or left, sometimes it's about taking the highway, sometimes it's a scenic country road, and sometimes it's about stopping. The speed is always the right speed; the traffic light is never wrong.

———

Take a breath when the light turns red. Relax your face, relax your features. Is there a better moment than this?

——

Darla Jean Folds Towels

——

Chop wood. Carry water.
Wash dishes. Sweep floors.
Scrub toilets. Fold laundry.
How does an enlightened person
live out her days?

KOAN

One evening, when Darla Jean was twelve, her mother taught her how to fold the freshly washed towels. While doing this, her mother asked, "Darla Jean, have you thought about what you are going to do when you grow up?"

Darla Jean said, "I'm going to make all the women happy."

Her mother doubled over with laughter.

Much later, Darla Jean's teacher said, "There is a treasure beyond happiness and unhappiness. How will you use it?"

REFLECTION

Like most children, Darla Jean was acutely aware of her mother's moods and feelings. When she was ten years old, her father had left them both. Darla Jean was very concerned about her mother's sadness at the divorce and at how hard her mother worked all day at the factory, came home, made their dinner, and then did the laundry. Darla Jean wanted her mother to be happy.

Folding towels is a simple household task that encompasses how life is to be lived. There is something about folding towels after washing them that I myself find satisfying and comforting to this day. Are you someone who is irritated with household chores or who hires someone to do them for you? If so, I encourage you to save one of these tasks for yourself and do it without a gap between you and washing dishes, folding towels, or mopping the floor.

When teaching about the precepts, the guidelines on how to live a wholesome life, my teacher, Bernie Glassman, would use the analogy of drinking from a glass. "You drink water from a glass, the glass gets dirty, so you wash the glass," he would say. In other words, getting things dirty is part of the very nature of living. So is cleaning them to use them again. Towels are of this cycle: you use the towels, the towels get dirty, you wash the towels, fold and put them away, and then use them again. The act of folding towels is infused with the intimacy of this cycle of daily life, an intimacy amplified when we are folding towels together with another person. It was in this way that Darla Jean and her mother folded towels one night after dinner, following a long day of work for her mother. Doing simple daily tasks together often gives rise to the sweet exchanges that anchor us in a householder life.

On this evening, Darla Jean's mother asked her, "Have you thought about what you will do when you grow up?" Darla Jean's response was unexpected: "I'm going to make all the women happy." Her mother doubled over with laughter. We may think this is a sweet and understandable sentiment for a child living in troubled circumstances, but for Darla Jean, this became a life vow. In that tender, unguarded moment, a great vow arose within Darla Jean out of deep resonance with all the women who suffer.

But what about this matter of happiness? One day a student from Switzerland visited my teacher and asked, "Maezumi Roshi, why is it that none of your students look happy?" Roshi was quite taken by this question. Relaying this conversation to me, he said, "I myself never think about whether I am happy. Egyoku, even if none of you are happy, I want some of you to at least *look* happy." Roshi and I doubled over with laughter. So, tell me, how about the one who is beyond the conditions of happiness? Does that person look happy?

Upon hearing about the time Darla Jean and her mother folded towels together, Darla Jean's teacher asked, "There is a treasure beyond happiness and unhappiness. How will you use it?" Plunge into the tasks at hand! Cast aside all thoughts and, if you are folding towels, empty into the folding, into the soft texture of the cloth, the fading of the colors, the running of your hands over the folds. Let yourself be enfolded. A small household task is, after all, not small at all.

———

How do you traverse the path that is beyond clean and dirty? A household task is a spiritual portal: How do you step through?

ROLAND:
Stepping Backward

"Now, here, you see, it takes all the running you can do to keep in the same place."[31]

KOAN

When Roland passed all his exams to become a doctor, he got sad, and even depressed. "There was no goal left, I felt useless. There was nothing driving me anywhere."

Many years later, combining a meditation and a homeopathic medicine practice, he says: "A step backward is a step forward; a step forward is a step backward."

REFLECTION

We are so goal oriented that life often appears to us as an arrow hurtling through the air to hit the bulls-eye. As long as we're on course, we're moving forward, but the minute we step off, if only to pause, it feels like we're falling back.

An old koan addresses this directly. Chao-chou once asked Nanquan Puyuan, "What is Tao?" Nanquan answered, "Ordinary mind is Tao." "Then should we direct ourselves toward it or not?" asked Chao-chou. "If you try to direct yourself toward it, you go away from it," answered Nanquan. Chao-chou didn't give up: "If we do not try, how can we know that it is Tao?"[32]

Isn't that what we naturally assume? If we don't try, how do we know that this really is it? If we don't set it up as a goal and then try our hardest, how will we get anywhere?

In Zen, we don't try to get anywhere. Our practice is about closing gaps, the gap between yourself and your Self, between you and me, between goal and practice, between the race and the finish line. "Tao does not belong to knowing or to not-knowing," Nanquan informs Chao-Chou. It does not lend itself to our daily bookkeeping of this + this + this = that. If you can plunge into each step, you will find the treasure right there. In fact, you don't have to go anywhere, you can find the treasure under your bare feet, right where you stand:

"Hundreds of flowers in spring, the moon in autumn,
A cool breeze in summer, and snow in winter;
If there is no vain cloud in your mind
For you it is a good season."

If you don't grasp at things, including goals and destinations, every day is a good day. That's fine, you might say, but we still need goals in life. Goals and priorities help us plan our day, but once we start an activity we can put away the internal clock, slow down our striving, let go of mental chatter, and let the flow take over. Most important, drop the inner voices that crowd our consciousness, pushing, imploring, warning us to shape up, work hard, get ahead.

We identify not just with our goal but also with activity. Many of us get up in the morning and go instantly into work mode. Are you one of those people made anxious by vacation, afraid you won't make up the time or lack of effort, that unopened emails and unanswered phone messages will accumulate, and you'll fall behind, miss out?

How could we miss out if, moment by moment, nothing's missing?

"Labor is a blessing, toil is the misery of man," Abraham Heschel, the twentieth-century Jewish philosopher, said in his book on the Sabbath.[33] These days, how many people take a full day off from checking emails? Taking a break feels like stepping backwards.

In Zen, we pay attention to the body-mind. The mind alone is full of thoughts and manic whispers, but when I consult the body-mind, the call may be to work, take time out, have a nap, go for a walk, pick up a book, or play with the dog. Whatever you choose to do, actually do it. Do you experience what you're doing or are you already thinking of the next step? Do you know where your feet and hands are at all times? A teacher can tell from students' body language as they come for face-to-face study whether they're ahead of themselves, their minds in forward motion, or whether they're centered and aware. Don't be propelled.

As Nanquan said to Chao-Chou: "Ordinary mind is Tao." Ordinary mind is the Way. There is nothing to make up, nothing to compete for, nothing to achieve. What in you does not believe that? What hungry ghost in you feels you must be more successful, more dedicated, more determined? That above all, you must always, always work harder? You cannot ignore or exclude this hungry ghost; it will not go away. If you try to feed it by working longer and longer hours, it will remain hungry and continue to tell you that something is always missing, that your life is still not it. Stop and listen carefully. Is anything really missing? Befriend the question. Befriend the ghost. Invite the ghost into the mandala of your practice and settle into the moment. Practice requires discipline and commitment, but not due to a sense of lack or failure. There is nothing to make up for.

Roland now says: "I am at home because I decided not to work anymore on Friday afternoon. The step backward is to be less successful and to get less money, but the step forward is to have more time for myself, for others, and for other parts of life. So, this step backward is a step forward!"

———

What have you considered a step forward in your life? A step backward? Have you lost anything from the first and gained anything from the second? If a step forward is a step backward, where do you land?

PATRICIA:
McTenzo Finds His Place

Cooking is dangerous work.
You can mistake the salt for sugar,
Maple syrup for soy sauce.
But the Iron Chef doesn't worry,
Her fixings have just one taste.

KOAN

One morning, Patricia opened the refrigerator and was astonished to find the Master sitting inside.

"What are you doing in there?" she asked.

"What are you doing out there?" the Master replied.

REFLECTION

I spend most of the hours of every day by a computer at my desk at home. Often, I look out the window at the road filled with cars, people, and animals, and imagine that life is out there rather than in here, where I am. In fact, whether I'm indoors or out, I usually experience a screen between the world and me, as though I'm watching life go by outside my window while I'm on the inside with lots of opinions about it.

People often say that when they find themselves too fixated on external things they take time out to focus their attention inwards. But is there an inside and an outside? Inside and outside of what?

The Gateless Gate is a well-known collection of Chan koans that are often referred to as gates of practice. When you see through one of those koans, you realize that there was no barrier to begin with, no shut gate. Householder koans are also gates of practice; in fact, each situation is a gate. If you are unattached to ideas and concepts of what things are or should be, you could go right through with no problem. Instead, we often embrace our own confinement.

I look outside the window and see the world; but tell me, isn't the world looking right back and seeing me? Who's looking in and who's looking out? Is there something that separates us? "Buddha Nature pervades the whole universe," we chant. No limits, no boundaries anywhere.

We may think that an inner life is one of meditation, reflection, and prayer, and that an outer life is everything else we do during the day. But in his famous instructions for meditation, Eihei Dogen wrote that meditation has nothing at all to do with sitting or lying down: "It is simply the Dharma gate of repose and bliss, the practice-realization of totally culminated enlightenment."[34]

What is this practice that promises repose and bliss? Can all aspects of our day—feeding our children, cleaning the house, answering the telephone, attending meetings, driving, doing bookkeeping, writing an article—be lived as "totally culminated enlightenment?"

We do so much without thinking about it. When you get dressed, do you consciously think out every detail? Do you work out how to put one arm into a sleeve, then the other, then the buttons, where the skirt goes or the pants, the socks and shoes? You probably get dressed without thinking about it, with no pause or confusion.

Isn't this repose and bliss, when things feel like they're self-accomplishing rather than a job that *I* have to do? When the purpose disappears into the activity, when both activity and purpose merge seamlessly, we call it "practice-realization." There's no criteria or measurement, we just do what needs to get done.

You might say that we relax into a purposeless, goal-less life. There are life's practicalities, of course, but our day-to-day life is its own purpose. We can let ourselves simply be and simply do, without all those self-conscious voices.

Practice *is* realization, practice *is* enlightenment. There is no other enlightenment.

———

How are you living your life right now? Is it inner or outer?

RYUDO:
Yesterday and Today

Don't be consistent.[35]

KOAN

While working in the V.A. hospital, Ryudo heard the following conversation:

"Nurse, did you give Mariah her meds this morning?"

"Yes, doctor, why do you ask?"

"Yesterday she was calm and focused, but today she is really out of control!"

REFLECTION

"Good morning," I say to a co-worker and get a bright smile in return. "Good morning," I say again to the same person the next day, expecting the same result. But this time my co-worker doesn't smile and I start worrying: *Is he feeling okay? Did something happen? Did I do anything wrong?* A subtle anxiety arises, a contraction, a slight shrinking away.

If something worked yesterday, shouldn't it work today, too? If the patient was fine yesterday, shouldn't he be fine today, too? But change and variation are everywhere, even in scientific experiments with strictly enforced controls. In fact, scientists now know that the very acts of observing and measuring data can alter outcomes.

We want things to be consistent and predictable. The smallest anomaly or disturbance in our routine—the lack of hot water in a morning shower, the dog messing up on the floor, the strange sound your car makes as you begin to drive—can throw off the entire day. You start looking for someone or something to hold on to, praying it stays the same and never changes: your husband, your wife, your child, your friend, your health.

They're all going to change.

Our resistance to change, the Buddha said, is the biggest factor behind our suffering. Take a moment to contemplate this. How do you feel when you see your children all grown up and ready to leave home, your job suddenly shifting, your spouse behaving differently than usual? Don't we fight tooth and nail against surprises and new turns of events?

My husband had a stroke, six days short of his seventy-seventh birthday. He'd been healthy and strong all his life. The massive stroke paralyzed the entire right side of his body as well as the speech center and other brain functions. For months, things were unstable and unpredictable, a blur of activity and intense emotions. They kept on changing all the time. "I'm looking for the new normal," I'd tell people, only the new normal was not

155

to be found. *Yesterday she was calm and focused, but today she's out of control.*

"Don't be consistent," was my husband's favorite Buddhist slogan. Life's not consistent. In fact, doesn't living according to our old routines feel like a life lived under glass? When the glass is shattered, there's a blast of cool air, and with it the raw freshness of being alive. We enjoy that sensation so much we immediately try to bottle it up, taking the same actions and expecting the same results, until the glass breaks once again and we discover that there's no new normal.

What do I depend on? All I have, all I ever have, is *now*. I can be completely present in this moment, or I can go into the stories in my head, sink into memories of how things were, get upset over how they've changed, and become apprehensive about the future.

Buddhist teacher Joan Halifax likes to say about her retreats and workshops, "The schedule is subject to reality." We can have any schedule we want, a daily regimen of greetings, medications, and appointments that remains the same one day after the next, but aren't they all subject to reality? Aren't they all subject to change?

You're not the person I married, you're not the person I knew. So tell me, who are you?

Dr. Ann Falls into a Trap

When you think you know, it's a trap.
When you don't know, it's a trap.
When you go beyond knowing and not-knowing, it's a trap.
Watch out!

KOAN

Before entering her new patient's room for the first time, Dr. Ann read his medical charts. Chet had an aggressive rectal cancer. He was not responding to chemotherapy and radiation treatments, his kidneys were obstructed by tumors, and he had returned to live with his parents because his wife could not care for him. She pictured an angry young man in a lot of pain from obstructed kidneys. As the medical expert, Dr. Ann decided that her new patient was ready for hospice.

Upon entering Chet's room, Dr. Ann was determined to carry out her plan. She said, "Good morning, Chet. How are you this morning?"

Chet greeted her with a big, beautiful smile. "Oh, so good, doc," he said. "That was the first night in months that I slept all night. I didn't have to get up to pee once!"

Dr. Ann experienced a shift.

REFLECTION

Does the attitude that you know exactly what is needed in a situation conceal what is right before you? This mindset of *I know what to do because I am the expert* or *because I just know better than you* is deeply ingrained; you are conditioned to know. Knowing can blind you to the ever-changing, ever-unfolding aspects of life. Not-knowing is not ignorance; it is life-affirming wisdom.

When Dr. Ann's new patient, Chet, flashed her a big, beautiful smile saying that he'd had the best night in months, his aliveness penetrated through Dr. Ann's authoritative knowing mind. In that moment, she experienced the living Chet. Tell me, what does it mean to know something? For many people, knowing often means figuring out a situation in their thoughts and then executing the plan. Do you approach situations and other people from your ideas of who they are and what is needed? This approach is guaranteed to fail, and yet, when it does fail, people are surprised, frustrated, and angry.

Knowing isolates and separates; not-knowing situates us in direct, intimate relationship to others and to the very nature of life. Not-knowing calls forth openness and deep listening, leading to a genuine connection without which you are apt to superimpose your ideas on others. Agendas, personal or professional, are hard to shake loose because they solidify the sense of who you are—*I am the expert, I can fix this, I know what is best.* Who I am is, in fact, permeable and not fixed at all. When confronted with *don't know*—or even a different point of view—can you recognize that the spaciousness of possibility has opened up, that more facets of life are being revealed? Or do you dig your heels into the mud and muck of what you know and insist that your way is the right way, dismissing the living ingredients that are right in front of you?

It's a common habit, albeit a limiting one, to reduce each other to a bundle of facts, information and opinions. This kind of knowing often ignores emotions, intuition or other aspects of life's mystery. Each of us is alive—a living being! You are not someone's idea of who you are; you are who you are. Other people are not your idea of who they are; they are who they are. Eyes seeing, ears hearing, nose smelling, tongue tasting, body touching, and consciousness are alive—vividly arising and passing away in unceasing movement.

It takes many years on the meditation cushion to be completely open to life as it is, not as you think it is. You may have had glimpses of not-knowing, just as when Chet's smile cut through Dr. Ann's agenda and she experienced a shift, a startling moment of aliveness, right here, now—*Who is this lying in the bed before me with a big, beautiful smile on his face?* The habitual knowing mind often quickly dismisses such insights. For Dr. Ann, however, this shift upended her usual functioning and marked the beginning of a lifelong spiritual practice of not-knowing.

Here, now, in this moment, can you rest in the space before any opinions are formed? To meet the present moment, set aside your knowing.

———

Demonstrate the intimacy of not-knowing. Show me your big, beautiful smile! Right now, present who you truly are.

MARTIN:
The Suffering of the World

"I am a refugee! I am an orphan! I am a homeless child!"
"The Buddha was right, life is suffering!"
"Who says I'm suffering?"

KOAN

Martin asked: How do I stop the suffering of the world?

REFLECTION

Martin is a doctor. His patients wait in the anteroom from morning to night to see him, recite what ails them, and get treatment for their pain. He is also a Zen teacher, and remembers a long time ago when he worked on a classic Zen koan: "Stop the sound of a distant temple bell. "[36] It was then, he says, that he became aware that his life koan was similar: How do I stop the suffering of the world?

Many of us have koans in the same vein: How do I stop the crying of my son? How do I stop my own suffering and pain?

How do I stop the wars, the misery of refugees, the hunger of children, and the mass extinction of species? And how do I stop being overwhelmed by a sense of powerlessness when I feel that I can't stop any of these?

We care about the world because we *are* the world. The Pietà, the Holocaust, the love of Romeo and Juliet, a puppy's playfulness, and the thousands of galaxies in the universe—these are closer to each of us than our dualistic brain can conceive.

Ordinarily, we don't experience ourselves that way, but aren't there hints? I am suddenly overwhelmed by a piece of art I saw for the first time today, it feels as intimate and familiar as my own hand. Or I hear of a terrible case of abuse and that moment, just as I feel revulsion and pity, there's a sense of déjà vu, of having experienced some of this myself, either as the abused or the abuser. I'm not talking about repressed memories, but rather an awareness of a strong and intimate kinship that can't be explained by the specifics of my life.

Over the years I've heard from a few people who've participated in our bearing witness retreats at Auschwitz-Birkenau that the place feels so close and familiar it's as if they'd been inmates there many years ago. These people have no family connection to what took place there, they're simply reporting what they experience.

Are you ever surprised by the emotional extremes you might sometimes feel in your small life? Isn't that because your life isn't small, because you may be fiercely aware of feelings and sensations that go beyond the labels of *my* experience, *my* life?

How do I stop the suffering of the world? Be the world. Be who you truly are.

If you're a doctor, that may mean listening to a patient describe his ailment as though it's *your* ailment, *your* pain. In a certain way, it is. For a journalist, it may mean giving voice to refugees as though she's the one escaping from terror and violence, not some stranger. For a lifeguard on the coast of Lampedusa, it may mean rushing into the waves and saving someone's small child in a leaky boat from the north coast of Africa because it's *his* child. For a receptionist welcoming a job applicant, it could be giving an encouraging smile and offering a cup of coffee because that's what he would want if he was sitting there hoping to get a job, not some outsider.

Are there outsiders? Are there strangers?

"We do not rescue anyone at the margins," wrote Fr. Greg Boyle, speaking of the gang members in southern California with whom he has worked for so many years. "But go figure, if we stand at the margins, we are all rescued. No mistake about it."[37]

Does stopping the suffering of the world require money or aid, or even entertaining the notion that you want to help people? Does it call for changing people around you for the better, or rather letting life work its way on you? Instead of going into a situation relying strictly on your knowing, with the agenda of fixing, repairing, and even healing, can you relax enough to let the situation mold and transform you? Can you accept the porousness of your own skin, the permeability of your mind? Can you accept that even the toughest of situations call for a quality of relaxation and even surrender, and trust in life as it is, unmitigated by personal viewpoints and agendas?

And don't forget, there's nothing small about "small acts of kindness." Can anyone know where the tiniest compassionate action will ultimately lead? How many people it will reach and how many lives it will change? We like to think of the one big action—and the one big leader—that can change the world. But as Taizan Maezumi Roshi used to say, small things aren't small.

You walk by a homeless man, introduce yourself and smile, and he fervently says, *Thank you so much!* Is that small? You help a lost little girl find her parent in the shopping center—is that small? You put out seeds for the birds during the cold winter season—is that small?

The suffering of the world is a specific situation, not some big abstraction. It calls us to do *this*, and *this*, and *this*. It calls us to get out of our heads and take concrete actions now, and now again, and now again.

———

You're stopped and asked for money on the street. What happens that moment? Are you aware of fear, anger, paralysis? Do you talk to the person? Walk away? Who's suffering? Do you have to know what to do ahead of time? Is there another way?

LOSS, ILLNESS, OLD AGE, & DEATH

ROBIN:

Unripe Fruit

If you've really lived,
Then you've already died many times—
Tick tock tick tock tick tock tick tock
Tick tock tick tock tick tock tick tock!

KOAN

Why does the fruit fall from the tree before it has ripened?

REFLECTION

Our time seems to come whether we're ready for it or not. Whether I'm eighteen or eighty, am I ever really ready? For that matter, am I ever really ripe? What does *ripe* feel like? Is it that I've fulfilled all my dreams? Is it that I've lived a happy life? Is it that I've aged gracefully, with a loving family beside me? Is it that the promises of my birth have all been creatively and joyously fulfilled?

For that matter, am I ever really ripe for anything—leaving home, getting married, having a baby, getting one job, getting another job, retirement, death? We have our life narrative: this happened, then this happened, then this happened, then this happened. One phase of life follows another in a nice, predictable fashion, each phase making us wiser by the day, like a pear that's green at the beginning, turns a tinge of pink, then a blush, a flush, and finally a ruddy, ready color. But life doesn't work like that. If anything, our mantra is usually: *Ready or not, here I come!*

"No creature ever falls short of its own completion. Wherever it stands it does not fail to cover the ground."[38] Life happens exactly as it's meant to. You might think it should have gone this way or that, should have been bigger, richer, or more important.

It's a sad day when someone tells me that he feels he hasn't really lived, that his life was full of obstructions: his parents, his upbringing, failures at work, troubles at home, so many unfulfilled promises. Or when someone belittles life generally: *Look at what's happened to this country! Young people didn't behave like this when I was growing up!* We bemoan our life and wish it were different, as though if we could change one thing—the right parent for the wrong one, the right spouse for the wrong one, making the right choice instead of the wrong one long ago—our life would be a lot happier. Is that really so?

"[I]f a bird or a fish tries to reach the limit of its element before moving in it, this bird or this fish will not find its way or its place. Attaining this place, one's daily life is the realization of ultimate reality."

Like the fish and the birds, none of us will ever investigate this entire earth. None of us will ever live out every possibility we ever faced or relive the many choices we make moment after moment. If we try, then like the fish and birds, we will not find our way or our place. Where do we find them? In our daily life, in the present moment.

What would it take to fully accept how our life has unfolded, and live it in contentment? Not think it should have been something else, or let other people tell us it should have been something else.

Surrendering to our life brings tremendous richness and depth. Zen Master Kosho Uchiyama wrote:

> *All of us are always living the "present moment"*
> *the profundity of the present moment*
> *Even when we don't know it and are blind to it*
> *the profundity of the present moment is embracing us as the*
> *present moment.*[39]

Eating an apple, walking the dog, cutting vegetables for soup, making the bed—all of these activities embrace us fully. That is so regardless of whether we experience it or not, so isn't it better to experience it? As Ben Connelly writes, "Countless unfathomable things are out of your control, but you always have the opportunity to give your best intention at this moment and thus plant seeds of happiness, kindness, and wellbeing for all things."[40]

We can complain and grieve; we can spend our days in regret. Or we can appreciate this unbelievably rare opportunity given us through birth, the result of innumerable events and processes unfolding over billions of years. Doesn't contemplating this just a little bit fill you with wonder, humbling and liberating all at the same time?

"This body does not belong to you, nor anyone else," said the Buddha.[41]

So what is this thing called *my life*? Is it just something private that starts at birth and ends at death? Could it also be *now* manifesting here in our bodies right now, a *now* that is beginningless and endless, an unimaginable gift? It's the body of liberation. How we walk, how we talk, how we meditate, how we are with others—is our only path to liberation; there is no other.

Working diligently with this body, with our life as it is, can we do our best?

———

What regrets about the past do you have? Do you think you wasted your life? Living your short lifespan with fullness and appreciation, moment by moment, is there waste or not?

KAREN:

The Old Woman Meets a Fish

The greatest thing is to give no fear.
How? Have no fear.
How? "With no hindrance of mind.
No hindrance, therefore no fear."[42]

KOAN

One night, Karen had this dream:

A young woman stepped out onto the path. She met a wolf. The wolf glowered, grinned, and growled. The woman ran.

This same woman, now a mother, again walked on the path. A bear appeared, bawling and beating his chest. The woman stood her ground and greeted the bear, and the bear ran.

The same woman, now gray-haired, drew near the wide, blue sea and saw a beautiful fish. But when she reached into the water to touch it, it became a roaring, flaming dragon that towered over her, flashing fierce, sharp teeth and steely spines. "Ah, teacher!" she said softly. At these words, the dragon wept salt tears.

REFLECTION

Karen adds: *As a young girl I wandered for hours by the ocean, lost in imagining the wild, mysterious, unknown creatures living in the sea. Now, I swim with them.*

Isn't one of the wonderful—and sometimes not so wonderful—things about growing older our seeing that we have become the very things we once feared or hated? We snap at our children, and a moment later realize that we're behaving like the mother or father we swore we'd never be. Ancient fears and nightmares plague us. Some of us are afraid of the dark even as we get older, or else we relive abuse that may have happened when we were children. Others seem to carry fears from previous generations: a buddy's death in the battlefield, a family catastrophe, pogroms and Nazi uniforms marching in goosestep. Add to that our now also being afraid of getting sick and growing old, being left alone, being the last one living.

A lifetime of fear.

It's only natural to want to run away. But if everything is one, then we're light, shadow, and everything in between. So what shadows do we escape from? What light do we run to? Every day presents me with answers to these questions. I look out my window and see leaves fall during autumn—do I get anxious at these seasonal signs of decline and death? I work less than I did before and am assailed by misgivings: Will I be good enough, valuable enough? Will anybody care? These are the monsters that have lived in our attic for many years. Can I be curious instead of fearful? Can I listen deeply to what life is showing me?

As we age we lose many of our defenses because we don't have the strength and energy to keep them up. What happens then? If we haven't worked with the wild and terrible things in our lives we can become more frozen and congealed than ever, mean and bitter. Working with them, don't I realize that their essence, like my own, is pure energy? When I constrict and turn away, I am also turning away from important sources of energy for my life.

For the Native Americans, animals are spirits that help people. They include scorpions, snakes, wolves, and bears. Practicing devotedly, living long enough with openness and courage, don't we experience ourselves as a circle of life, including wolf, bear, fish, and dragon? There are fewer icons and pedestals, and also fewer enemies. In T. S. Eliot's words:

> *We shall not cease from exploration*
> *And the end of all our exploring*
> *Will be to arrive where we started*
> *And know the place for the first time.*[43]

What would it be like, to know the place where we started for the first time?

A little like the hero of Homer's *Odyssey*, we leave home, love, struggle, battle with monsters, face temptations and impossible situations, lose loved ones, lose our way, and—if we're lucky—finally come home. Can't we experience old age as finally coming home? Even though our skin is more wrinkled, don't we feel more comfortable in it? Even as our bones ache, haven't we learned the limits of things? Don't we feel our parents deep inside us because we are their age now? And don't we face mistakes—ours and others'—with more equanimity now, realizing that they may not have been mistakes at all?

We've faced the wolf, the bear, the fish, and the dragon; we know they're us. We're finally comfortable with all our different forms and shapes, be they the child, the adult, or the old man or woman.

Can I know this place today? Can I know it every day? Do I have to wait until I've accumulated the wisdom of old age? There is a way to know and claim it this minute. By now you know how. You can encounter the bear, wolf, and dragon with a beginner's mind at any age. Do curiosity, openness, and optimism just belong to children, or are they available to us any time, even now?

———

What dangerous animals have you met on your journey? Are you afraid of them now, too? What has changed? Are there new fears that have arisen instead?

JITSUJO:
Hard Work

Breathing in, breathing out.
Is it hard, is it easy?
When it is time to die,
The breath stops by itself.

KOAN

Jitsujo was with her father in his hospital room when the machine he was hooked up to started beeping wildly. Seeing his labored breathing, she latched her hands onto his chest, locked eyes with him, and completely lost herself in his breathing: *ahhhhh ... uuuuuuu* ... continuously, in perfect harmony.

Suddenly her father said, "It's hard work, isn't it?"

REFLECTION

Being with a person who is dying, especially when it is your own father, is hard emotional work. Paying keen attention at the

175

bedside, you listen with your entire being to what is unfolding before you, moment by moment. Your breath can harmonize so acutely with the dying person's that at the first sign of difficulty, you spontaneously jump in to help the person breathe. So it was for Jitsujo.

Breathing is mysterious. What is this breath that your body inhales and exhales moment by moment? Zen teachers giving instruction to students say, "When you breathe in, breathe in the whole universe. When you breathe out, breathe out the whole universe. Your entire body breathes. The entire universe breathes. Just breathe in this way."

Right now, how are you breathing? Where does your breath begin? Where does it end? An Ancient One said, "Breath enters your body, yet there is nowhere from which it comes. Breath leaves the body, yet there is nowhere to which it goes. Therefore, it is not long or short."[44] It is not only the nose or the lungs that breathe, it is your entire body that breathes. Every pore of the body is breathing this one continuous breath. Just inhaling! Just exhaling!

When Jitsujo saw how labored her father's breathing was, she sprang into action and synchronized her breathing with his. *Ahhhh*—breathing in, *uuuuuu*—breathing out, over and over. In this most intimate way, their breathing became one. Sharing breath affirms your fundamental connection with another person.

When my good friend was dying, those of us around him were so attentive to his breathing that at the time of his last breaths, all of us, in unison, inhaled, were suspended between breaths, and then took his final exhale with him. It was as though the entire universe was breathing one breath—we were all being breathed and being expired together.

When your body functions smoothly, you are not conscious of its functioning. Your brain cells fire, the blood flows, the heart pumps, the lungs expand and contract with each breath. But when you have a chronic lung condition or when you are dying, like Jitsujo's father was, there is a greater awareness of the breath. What was once second nature suddenly requires great effort.

In meditation, breathing harmonizes all parts of your own being. When you meditate with others, everyone's breathing harmonizes effortlessly and weaves the web of who we are together. With each breath, you are weaving and being woven with the whole universe. In this way, you, the great earth, and all beings are sustaining each other's lives. All are breathing air. All are inhaling and exhaling together. Learn to breathe well by harmonizing with the natural contraction and expansion of the great rhythm of life. So tell me, how are you receiving the breath of others? Of the whole universe? Of birth and death?

Jitsujo's father said, "It's hard work, isn't it?" At the moment when death was near, with these tender words, her father expressed his love for her. You cannot die for me, I cannot live for you—but here, right now, this very breath is shared intimately. How about it?

It's hard work, isn't it?

How is the one continuous breath manifesting in this very moment?

SHUNRYO:
My Mother's Diaper

I'm my mother's daughter; I'm my mother's mother.
Is one truer than the other?
Calling things dual or nondual
Will just add more waste to what you carry.

KOAN

Two years into being my mother's primary caregiver, she began to need adult diapers. She adapted to them without comment. For me, the ritual of sitting on the edge of the tub first thing in the morning, facing mom as she's seated on the toilet, sliding her pants and diaper first over her knees, and then off each foot, has become a meditation.

How heavy is my mother's diaper?

REFLECTION

For twelve years, during my adolescence and early adulthood, my mother was institutionalized for mental illness. She was self-destructive, with multiple attempts at suicide; she cut herself and tried to break her bones by bashing them against whatever hard surface she could find. She alternated between smoldering silence, deep-voiced threats, and outright rage. Thorazine, extensive anti-depressants, electroshock, and years of psychoanalysis at Pennsylvania's finest institution didn't help. When Mom tried to come home, we were told to never let her out of our sight in case she'd try to buy razors or pills or do something drastic.

When she went back to the institute, we were called in to a family meeting. Mom's psychiatrist coached my mother to reveal that we would not be allowed to go out with her alone anymore. "I sometimes have urges to kill you."

My mother suffered deeply and perpetrated a lot of suffering onto her children. My brother and I nearly died many times, each battling our own addictions. Being her primary caregiver now for five years, with my brother helping as he can from afar, I have come to be aware of my love for my mother for the first time in years.

What is past? What is present or future? When we think that something has already happened, we conclude that there's nothing we can do about it anymore, past is past. Seeing everything as now, happening and manifesting simultaneously, gives a different meaning to my actions. I become aware that nothing is said and done once and for all, everything is dynamically affected by everything else, so the action I take now is very important.

Tell me, whose diaper is this anyway? My mother's? My grandmother's? My own?

Doesn't taking care of a person who may have hurt you transform your life in unimaginable ways? Reflect that this is the person who gave you life. They carried you inside their own bodies, they went through the pains of labor to give you birth, fed you, and took care of you when you couldn't do this for yourself.

Does it mean they had parenting skills as we know them now? Does it mean they were knowledgeable, loving, even sane? Does it mean they may not have had their own lifetime of fierce struggle?

A woman was the first to get higher education in her family. When she went to college, her mother said to her: "Please don't come back and analyze us."

Can we grasp that our parents are their own people with identities other than *parents*, that in fact we're in their lives only a relatively short while? Doesn't seeing that enable you to let go of your identity as *child*, thus freeing both you and your parents to be adults?

When we become the ones now taking care of our elderly parents, it feels as though a role reversal is taking place, and for many this is a difficult time. The attention you got or didn't get as a child, the care and love you received or missed, all these now go to the parent you once loved beyond all measure, hated beyond all measure, and everything in between. A lot goes through our mind: stories, memories, vignettes, childhood scenes. What will draw you back to the present? *How heavy is my mother's diaper?*

Once it was your diaper; now it's your mother's, or your father's. But always, it's a diaper. Feel the heaviness, smell the smell, help her/him put it on and take it off, make sure a new one is within reach. Your roles have changed, everything feels different. Still and always, there's a diaper that's being changed, the act of keeping clean, of taking care of the body. Whose body is it?

When I'm changing diapers, I'm also changing the world, taking part in the ceaseless task of caring for the One Body. Is there any other body?

The most mundane tasks, given attention, become sacred. Putting diapers on a parent can become a sacrament. Even if your heart and mind are elsewhere, even if they still dwell in old angers and resentments, your hands are already beginning the work, cleaning and dressing, ministering to your parents' old and tired bodies. One day you sit on the edge of the tub, letting go of old thoughts and recollections, pay attention to the business of changing diapers, and realize that the work of healing has already begun.

Each night I used to put salve on my husband's right arm, shoulder, hand, and leg, affected by stroke. Slowly, the yellow salve streamed between the fingers and onto the pale, thin skin. Tell me, whose body was I attending to? His? Mine? The Buddha's?

When parents come around, who takes care of whom? How attached are you to still being the child? You may still be a child in stories and memories, but where are you the grown-up?

Greg's Body

"Are you old?"
"I guess I am."
"Are you going to die?"
"I guess I am, but not yet."
"Don't worry, you'll do it really good."

KOAN

Greg had struggled for decades with post-traumatic stress disorder since being stabbed with a nine-inch knife in the 1960s at the age of sixteen. Thirty-five years later, when meditation practice and psychiatric treatment had finally begun to stop the horrific flashbacks that had tormented him for so long, Greg's doctor told him he had terminal cancer and would die within the year.

Upon hearing this diagnosis, Greg asked, "What will become of my body?"

REFLECTION

When we become ill, we realize that we're not that important. There are projects to work on, deadlines to meet, families to attend to, and instead we have to lie in bed and rest. Does the world stop? It does not. The work finds a way to go on, or else it doesn't. At home, the kids may be disappointed, but they too continue to live their lives. We're like snowflakes: highly individualized, exquisitely designed, and melting away almost as soon as we hit the ground.

What will become of my body? In fact, who and what is this body that fades and weakens, turns pale, doesn't want to get up in the morning, aches, loses appetite, looks out the window for hours at a time, finds it hard to focus on simple things, feels hot, feels cold, gets pain attacks, can't sleep, becomes feeble? Is this body *me?*

Once, this body was the good parent, the successful breadwinner, the aspiring musician or painter, the disciplined jogger, the sexy man or woman who at times felt on top of the world. Now this body can't feed, wash, or toilet itself; evokes expressions of pity on people's faces; and is ignored by the staff members of a nursing home or hospital. Its food preferences can't be indulged, its beautiful clothes are replaced by hospital gowns, the independence it was proud of is gone like yesterday's rain, and one self-image after another drops into the wastebasket of irrelevance.

What is this body? Who am I?

This had been Greg's question not just once, but over a lifetime. In that lifetime he seemed to get blindsided again and again. Isn't that true for many of us? You work hard all your life and look forward to a leisurely retirement, only to get bad news from your doctor. It's one hardship after another—your mother is ill,

183

your husband is fired from his job, a fire burns down your house—and still you assure yourself that there's light at the end of every tunnel and everything will turn out okay in the end. The truth is, one never knows.

Bearing witness never ends. One day your heart won't break, you tell yourself. You won't suffer anymore; you'll finally achieve equanimity thanks to your deep meditation practice. As if Nirvana is some numbed-out state where nothing hurts, nothing scratches, and you wear a smile on your face day in, day out.

Or else you look for resolution. One day it'll become clear, everything will make sense, and you'll be able to tell the story of how it all went down and how much you learned and realized towards the end of your life. *One day one day*, as Rabbi Shlomo Carlebach loved to say. We spend a lot of time creating such stories.

Sometimes we think we've found our life's meaning while mountain-climbing, or in a poem or during a retreat, out of which a deep sense of clarity and balance emerges that we believe nothing, but nothing, will ever upset again. But the very next day that hard-won story or meaning doesn't feel so relevant anymore, and we're back to the old question: So who am I? What will happen to my body?

The Buddha didn't address questions such as an afterlife, or what happens after death. He came out of an Indian culture that believed in reincarnation, but the Great Physician's teachings focused on suffering and delusion: how they arise, and how they can end. But in the *Lotus Sutra*, one of the most famous of Buddhist sutras, the Buddha says that he has been teaching people how to awaken for millions of years, though historically it's only been some two and a half thousand years: "In order to save living beings, as an expedient means I appear to enter nirvana but in truth I do not pass into extinction, I am always here, preaching the Law."[45] Due to their delusions, people don't see him. But when the time comes, and suffering beings thirst for his teachings, he reappears to teach again.

How is this possible? The Buddha was a vessel for teaching and transformation. He died in his eighties, but he continues to be that vessel many generations later. His body was cremated, but what was his essence, and where did it go? Isn't each of us a vessel for transformation?

That is what Greg was asking, and maybe what many of us ask as well. Once our bodies go, then what? There is much we don't know, but one thing is clear, and that is that the results of our actions go on and on. The Buddha, Christ, Mohammed, Moses, and the Iroquois Peacemaker all lived and taught for a relatively short time, but the effects of those lives continue to resonate everywhere.

The value of our actions is immeasurable, and it transcends our human lifespan. Do we have to be among the world's great teachers? Any moment now, we come face to face with a child needing boots for winter, an animal hit by a car on the road, someone needing help to pay the rent or get a job. Doesn't our response live on, not just in our life, but also in our family, our community, and in the world?

Are you concerned about the future? If so, what is your practice now? Where will your body go?

KANJI:

A Good Death, a Bad Death

How do we live according to the teachings of the Buddha? Get born and die every day.

KOAN

Kanji's father lay dying in a hospital room, feeble yet still alert. Kanji hoped to give him the final gift of a good death. The two embraced, kissed, and said they loved each other. Kanji said to himself, *This is a good death.*

The next day, after his father became unconscious, gasping for breath, other members of the family sat near the bed chatting about news and trivia, laughing and sharing irrelevant stories. Kanji told himself, *This is a bad death.*

That night everyone left the room except Kanji and his exhausted mother, who slept in a chair near the bed. All night Kanji stayed awake, holding his father's hand and whispering comforting words in his ear. Kanji thought, *This is a good death.*

The next day his father was comatose. Kanji stood near the hospital bed, listening to other family members talking. Suddenly his father shouted—a groan of agony, face clenched in pain, body arched and rigid in intense suffering. Then he lay still. The heart monitor plunged to zero.

Kanji experienced an opening.

REFLECTION

Sometimes people think that spirituality smoothens things out, makes good and bad equally tolerable, maybe even nice. Or else it takes us beyond into some holy, transcendent space. We hide behind concepts such as oneness, emptiness, and enlightenment; we talk about the spirit world.

Doesn't this stand out most strikingly at a time of death? Death scares us worse than anything. That's when we use words and phrases like: *she left her body, he has gone to the other shore, she has left this realm of existence, he is now in heaven, she has gone to God*. Most of the time the work of disposing of the corpse is done by surrogates: undertakers to handle the body, chemicals to hide the disintegration and cover up the smell, crematoria operators to burn the body or gravediggers to bury it.

In a Zen Buddhist memorial service, we invoke the *vast ocean of dazzling light* and *tranquil passages of great calm*, but doesn't the actual experience feel very different? There's the smell of illness and medications, urine, and disinfectant. There's groaning and struggling, or a morphine-induced haze fading into unconsciousness or coma.

Is there any way to make death neat or clean? Can we predict how and when death will come, whether in a car accident, a sudden heart attack, a lingering illness, violence, or old age? If anything, death is a showcase for how vulnerable we are, how we hang on to life by only the thinnest of threads, how inexorable and inevitable the end of our life really is. No one, not the most loving son or daughter, not the best physician in the world, can save us from it.

As more and more volunteers have gotten involved in hospice and the care of the dying, we hear of deathbed scenes full of peace and love, with no anguish, pain, regrets, or struggle, and we think: *That's what I want for myself, for my loved ones, for my friends. I want a good death.* We make preparations, write Living Wills and designate Health Care Proxies. We think about how we'd like to die—what prayers or book passages should be recited, what music should be played—and have clear discussions about this with our families and loved ones.

But in the end the heart monitor will plunge to zero. The relationships that have depended on this heart will end, as will the thinking and planning that have depended on our brain. Since we don't know how this will happen, the preparations we made may be effective or not. We may have wanted all our family members to be with us, but our death happens so fast that only First Responders are there. We may have decided not to take extraordinary measures to prolong our life, not to eat or drink, and in the end change our mind.

I can't control the terms of my death, but what about how I meet it? Can I even label it as *good* or *bad*?

A friend of mine, a psychiatrist and longtime Zen practitioner, lay in hospice in his ninety-first year and grumbled: *Why is it taking me so long to die?*

Death is simple—and sacred—beyond words.

A new journey begins and ends in a flash, followed by another journey, and another one after that because each moment you die and are reborn. We judge this moment good, that one bad, another indifferent. Isn't that like saying that this life is good, another is better, the one after that not so good? Change is perpetual, but so is connection. We breathe in air and breathe it out again, and the air we breathe out others in the room breathe in while we breathe in the air they just expelled from their lungs. So much connects us all the time.

No matter what or how much I murmur to my dying father, the basic connection was made long ago. The elements of his life are intertwined with mine and mine with his. Doors are opening and closing all the time; change and connection are an inextricable part of every moment.

"Buddha's relics are body and mind," we chant at a memorial service. Is anything truly gone?

I will hold his hand, give him a drink of water, and apply a cool, wet towel to his hot face. The memorial chant says: "Vast ocean of dazzling light, marked by the waves of life and death; the tranquil passage of great calm embodies the form of new and old, coming and going. We devoutly aspire to true compassion."

Tell me, what is true compassion?

———

Think of when you were at the bedside of someone who died. Was it a good or a bad death? In whose judgment? What made it one or the other?

ENJU:
The Infinite Black Abyss

Aaiiiiiieeeeeeeeee!
When the great scream
Resounds throughout the whole universe,
Place your palms together and bow your head.

KOAN

Enju's husband and their only child, thirteen-and-a-half-year-old Seth, were visiting Seth's grandparents in Florida. Her husband returned home early, and when it was time for Seth to fly home a few days later, he boarded his flight. On his way home, the plane crashed in Denver. Seth was killed.

Of this time, many years later, Enju says, "An infinite black abyss opened, and a force shoved my head into it. I plunged into a blackness that is always here, but you don't have to relate to it, if you are lucky."

Her teacher said, "Enju, there is a Jizo Bodhisattva in the garden that needs a new cape."

REFLECTION

A devastating loss. Unbearable grief. A blow that obliterates you completely. There are small changes in life that are easily negotiated, and then there are sudden, catastrophic upheavals of such magnitude that the life you have known is no more. Loss consumes you.

The Buddha saw that everything is in constant flux. My teacher, Maezumi Roshi, liked to say that "we are being born and dying six and a half billion times every twenty-four hours."[46] Then he would ask, "How can you live such a life?" "And yet," he would reply, "you *are* living it." This transiency is called birth-and-death. Zen Master Dogen writes that birth and death are the life of the Buddha. My Zen teacher taught that such a life has different dimensions: There is the conventional birth-and-death, in which we were born one day, are living now, and one day will die; there is the spiritual birth-and-death in which self-centeredness diminishes and the awakened mind comes to the fore; and there is the life-and-death of each moment. The journey of grief encompasses all of these.

Kisagotami lived at the time of the Buddha. When her little child died, she lost her mind with grief. She carried his lifeless body to Shakyamuni Buddha and begged him to bring her child back to life. The compassionate and wise Buddha said, "First, bring me a mustard seed from a house that has not known death." Kisagotami carried her dead child from house to house in her village, moving among people she undoubtedly knew and who knew her and her child. They invited her in, offered tea, and bore witness to her grief. Not finding one household that had not known death, she began to accept that death is what is. You know this,

191

and yet you don't quite know it until it happens to your child, to someone close to you, or to you yourself.

You expect things to be a certain way rather than how they actually are: a child dying before his parents, or a spouse before yourself. Nor do you expect to become suddenly seriously ill, or lose your main source of income, or watch your house and belongings gathered over a lifetime burn to the ground. There is no end to the kind of losses you may endure. You may even lose your mind, as Kisagotami did. Isn't that one of your biggest fears, the unraveling of your life's narrative?

The death of a child is a searing loss that no one should ever have to endure, and yet people do. When a heart is shattered in this way, there is only *this,* and words that are achingly hard to utter. There is also the healing power of kindness. Enju and her husband were surrounded by good, caring friends who supported them through countless acts of kindness. First were all the many immediate tasks that needed doing. Then there was the living through, moment by moment, one foot in front of the other. After a few months had passed, a friend introduced them to a rabbi, who over many more months sat with Enju and her husband, receiving them just as they were and listening deeply to their grief.

Can you yourself hold the space for someone else's suffering? Being witnessed is so crucial for healing on every level. Kisagotami's healing likely began when her neighbors invited her into their homes and bore witness to her grief. The good rabbi did not turn away from Enju and her husband, a couple he did not previously know. Do you have the capacity to hold the space for such pain, when being the listener can take you to your own edges?

Grief has its own fierce force; there is no right or wrong way to grieve. Even within a family, each person's grief journey is unique to him/herself. How do you live with these individual rhythms of grief, however they manifest for you or for someone you know?

Enju said: "An infinite black abyss opened, and a force shoved my head into it." What is this infinite black abyss? What is this place of infinite bottomless darkness, this unrelenting, universal life force that claims us to our essence? In Zen, the emptying out of the self is called the Great Death. This is a spiritual death, a self-shattering experience in which there is only timeless infinity. Zen master Keizan Zenji, describing his own experience, said, "A black ball rushes through the black night."[47] I recall one of my teachers saying, "Nowhere, nobody."

Enju herself said, "I plunged into a blackness that is always here, but you don't have to relate to it, if you are lucky." The loss of a child calls forth a deep surrender, which can lead to profound openness and vulnerability. In her book *Bearing the Unbearable,* Joanne Cacciatore writes: "While grieving the death of someone loved will last a lifetime, if we are able to remain close to our original wound, honestly, being with it and surrendering to it, we can experience a kind of transcendence, a transfiguration."[48]

An ancient koan asks: "How is it when a person who has died the great death returns to life?" The Zen master replies, "You must not go by night, you must go by day light."[49] The life force is unrelenting even in the midst of great loss: The sun rises and warms the earth, new green shoots poke through black lava beds, and a tiny pink bud appears on a bare branch. At the same time, rebirth does not obviate death. Today, Enju and her husband are parents to two beautiful adopted daughters.

At the Zen Center of Los Angeles, a hand-carved stone statue of Jizo Bodhisattva, the great being that takes care of children after death, sits below the winter pear tree among the delicate irises. It sports a red cape knitted by Enju, who tends to the Jizo in memory of Seth. Now and then, one sees that a fallen leaf has been tucked lovingly into the folds of his cape.

How are you tending to life-and-death, moment by moment?

———

When everything falls apart, what then? What has emerged for you from great loss? The infinite black abyss—what is it?

Betsy's Mom Asks, "Whatcha Doing?"

I will tickle your ribs
with my breath.
I will catch your tears
with my heart.
What activity is this?

KOAN

Betsy's mom asked her, "Whatcha doing?" Before she could respond, her mom said, "Hee hee. I am not over there anymore." Betsy looked over, saw her mother's corpse, and let out a great laugh.

REFLECTION

What is dead? What is alive?

There is an old Zen story about a master and his disciple who attend a funeral together to pay their respects to the deceased. When they arrive, they walk up to the corpse, and the disciple hits the coffin with his hand, and asks, "Is this dead? Is this alive?" The master says, "I won't say, I won't say."[50]

What do you say? Don't be quick to respond.

Betsy's mom had been unresponsive for days. Betsy would spend the night with her head resting on the side of her mother's bed and her hand on her mother's shoulder so that she could feel her breathing. Betsy had the sensation of being a puppy, curled up next to its mother. This closeness healed something deep within her.

If you have kept a vigil beside a dying person, you know that what is conventionally called *dying* is very much alive. Dying is a vividly lived experience for both the dying person and those keeping watch. Today so much is written about this, but when you keep vigil with someone who is dying, you relinquish, or at least set aside, your own ideas about death. The great mystery itself is so immediate that it commands you into its presence just as it is.

Isn't it amazing to think that one day your breath and your very heart will stop? You won't be here anymore. Occasionally, my teacher would say, "If you really understood impermanence, you wouldn't be able to take it." You know you will die, but you don't quite know it either, not even when you are sitting at the bedside of someone dying.

If you want to know about dying, don't ask a Zen master. She will say things like, "I don't know, I'm not dead yet." Or: "When you die, just die."

The next morning, sitting by her mother's bedside, Betsy felt deeply peaceful. She was reading a book, pondering a sentence, when suddenly she heard her mother ask playfully, "Whatcha doing?" "Hee hee," her mother laughed as Betsy bolted upright.

"I'm not over there anymore." Startled, Betsy laughed and said, "MOM!" She looked over at the bed and saw her mother's dead body. Betsy shook her head, smiled, and said, "I love you, mom." She could feel her mother say "I love you" back to her as her mother's energy headed out the door.

This corpse, is it dead? Is it alive?

Betsy had a chant with her for the moment when her mother would die. She began to chant, but then hesitated. *Should I chant this?* she wondered. *Does my mother need these instructions? Doesn't she know more than I do at this moment?* Then she felt her mother scolding her, "Seriously now, Betsy, you're a priest." Her mother laughed. "You finish that chant."

But tell me, where is Betsy's mother now?

The rational mind likes to create its scenarios about dying. You will die however you die. You may witness someone's life come to an end and yet have no access to what this process of dying really is. The great mystery calls forth a unique and deeply personal response from each of us, and we don't know ahead of time what it will be.

There is a death poem by Zen Master Ikkyū:

I won't die,
I won't go anywhere,
But I won't be here.
So don't ask anything—
For I won't answer![51]

Or will you?

———

Are you alive? Are you dead while alive? How do you live knowing you will die? Show me! How does your view of dying affect the way you are living now?

Helga Sees Her Own Death

Be respectfully reminded: time swiftly passes by
And opportunity is lost.
Today, the days of your life are decreased by one.
Do not squander your life.[52]

KOAN

Helga had a realization and her eyes grew as wide as saucers. "I just now realized that I am going to die," she said.

The person next to her looked into her eyes and said, "Yes, Helga, you are going to die."

Helga's eyes grew even wider.

The person said, "You are in the right place."

Helga replied, "Thank you, thank you."

REFLECTION

As Helga aged and slowed down, she returned to her spiritual practice, including daylong retreats. During one such retreat, the reality of her own mortality hit her like a ton of bricks.

Have you known this visceral moment when you realize that your own death is no longer in the far future or no longer just an idea? The certainty of your own death—that there will be a time when your body-mind will no longer exist at all, when your breath will cease, when there will not be another heartbeat—is an acutely physical experience. Indeed, Helga's eyes grew wide as saucers.

You can wax philosophical or pontificate about death all you wish, but the fact remains that you will not live in your skin one day. You will not be able to do any of the things that occupy your life right now, nor will you be able to do anything for anyone. How can you live awake to the fact that your own death may happen at any moment?

Although we usually think that we were born, are now alive over certain years, and one day we'll die, we are actually being born and dying all the time. Zen teachers tell us that birth-and-death repeats itself in every moment, again and again, forever.

We can hone this sense of continually being born and dying by consciously practicing it over and over. For instance, when you are weeding in your garden, be aware of being born in your garden. When you are done weeding, die and be reborn putting your gardening tools away. When you are taking your shower, be aware of being born in the shower. Die stepping out of the shower and be born drying yourself with a towel, and so forth. Set aside time to do this practice during your day.

You can do the same practice each time you change roles. For instance, you are born as a friend one moment, as a parent an hour later, and as a co-worker after that, dying in one role and being born in another. In daily life, you move from role to role so rapidly that it seems like one continuous stream, which you call *me, myself.* When consciously examining this matter of birth and death, ask yourself: Who is this that is being born and dying so rapidly and continuously?

As she approached eighty years of age, Helga was suddenly struck by the reality of her own death. But could she see the reality of being born and dying moment by moment? Can you? The person whose arm Helga grabbed looked deeply and steadily into her eyes and affirmed her realization. "Yes, you will die." Then the person added, "You are in the right place."

Tell me, what is this "right place?"

Here, now, is the right place for your life to happen. Here, now, is the right place for your death to happen.

"Thank you," Helga said. "Thank you, thank you."

Truly, there is nothing like an affirmation of reality to set you free. Yes, you and I are going to die. What about it?

———

Being born and dying every moment, how are you living this reality right now?

———

VIVIANNE:
Blaming God

———

"Speak what you perceive to be the truth
Without guilt or blame."[53]
But even in the midst of guilt and blame,
In the sticky swamp of anger and complaint—
Right there is a path.

KOAN

Vivianne told her teacher: "For myself, I know that God does not exist. Nevertheless, I am very angry at him for taking away my parents much too early."

REFLECTION

An old friend used to say that Zen practitioners talk a lot about no-self and impermanence, including the lack of any permanent soul, but the moment tragedy hits, they pray to God.

Or else they blame God. When something unexpected and painful happens, don't we invoke the presence of an omnipotent being whom we could blame? More generally, whenever the gap appears between life as it is and life as we think it should be, between people as they are and people as they should be, don't we often need to name someone, or Someone, as the responsible party? In that gap lie our anger, disappointment, and blame, accompanied by feelings of weakness and helplessness. In a dualistic paradigm, weakness and helplessness find their opposite match in authority, power, and control.

When we ascribe these latter qualities to the Unknown, we are making of it a mirror image of ourselves, giving it the opposite qualities of those we take on. Psychologists call it projection; some spiritual teachers call it idolatry.

Many mystical traditions have defined God as that which can't be known. Not-knowing is the source of all manifestations, including things like the death of loved parents, children, animals, and anything we hold dear. But when tragedy hits, doubt rears its formidable head: *How is it possible? How could it happen?* When things fall outside our conceptual understanding of what's right and wrong, what's justified and what's not, isn't it common to point to some being to whom we ascribe omnipotence and say: *How could You do this?*

We don't have to believe in God to behave this way. All we have to do is keep company with grievances and indignation, and repeat to ourselves our favorite monologues concerning disappointed loves and dashed hopes, accidents and tragedies. Does life care one bit? Can all the vigilance in the world, including praying to and invoking the protection of a divine being, prevent bad things from happening?

203

So what helps? First, take a breath. Pay attention to how your body lives without asking for permission, how it lives even when deep inside you want to die. Drink a cup of tea. Inside you feel raw and grief-stricken, sure you'll never be happy again, but when you pay attention, notice what comfort you took from drinking the hot tea, how each swallow settled and calmed you.

Continuing to pay attention, you may later notice that your face softens while watching the sun set, that you stroke the dog as it nuzzles against you, and that though you didn't have much appetite for dinner you enjoyed the blueberries. In those moments is there grief alone, or also hot tea, a sunset, a dog, blueberries? The point isn't to deny the loss, just not to stay in the story of the loss. When I stay with the loss itself, there is plenty of sorrow and heartbreak, but there's also the feel of a hot bath or the shock of cold night air when I go out.

"How are you doing?" someone asks. If I'm answering from my story, I might say: "I can't stop crying." If I've been paying attention, I might answer: "I cry a lot, smell flowers, feel a terrible sadness, talk to someone I love on the phone, look up at the sky, cry again, watch TV, sleep." Sadness arises in the moment, joy arises in the moment, as do surprise, sorrow, pain, peace, and everything else. In my head I'm sure I've been mourning relentlessly for weeks, even months, but when I pay attention, I see that the stirrings of life haven't gone away. At first they're muted and subtle, but when I shine the light of attention on them, they are unmistakably there.

There is another practice to be cultivated here. "I need to be reminded that most people out there carry far bigger burdens in a more humble and noble manner than I ever will; have forgiven far more; have contained far more; have had to come to more peace with life than I ever will have to," wrote Fr. Greg Boyle, founder of Homeboy Industries, serving gang members in Los Angeles. "It is literally mind-blowing to live with that again and again."[54]

Pain and loss are everywhere. When they hit us, it may feel natural to implode and collapse inside. But are you the only one who has lost parents suddenly, come down with cancer, or gotten hurt in a car accident? Millions have. Can you feel that?

It's important to practice ahead of time. When something joyous happens in your life, you can say to yourself: *I am happy; may everyone be happy.* When you're enjoying a glorious summer afternoon, you might say: *I am having a beautiful day; may everyone have days like this one.*

It may feel contrived at first, but you're practicing expanding your personal universe to include more and more people, more and more beings. You're bearing witness to how we mix with and penetrate everyone and everything through our experiences. It's natural to feel your own loss worse than anyone else's, but by including the universe in joys and sorrows, you are practicing to become more supple, more aware of the flow of emotional energy. You participate in the joys and sufferings of the world, and the world participates in your joy and suffering.

Another name for this is grace. Do you have to live and work in the gang neighborhoods of Los Angeles, like Greg Boyle, to be amazed by people's strength? Haven't you learned by now that the neighbor across the street, the newly-arrived immigrant you greet at the grocery store, and the caregiver ministering to your father have dealt with tragedies and losses that defy imagination, and still they smile at you, greet the day, raise their children, take care of life? Do they look like heroes?

When you learn their names and listen to their stories you are plowing the field, developing an inner culture of reaching out and connection. In that way, when loss finally happens in your life, it will affect you more than others, but will it be yours alone?

You may find that the world grieves with you.

———

"I've been sad all day. I'm a neurotic mess. I'm a manic-depressive." *Tell me, right now, where are your feet and hands? Did you have breakfast? Did you wash the dishes? Do you hear the play of wind chimes outside?*

MANY
GATES OF
PRACTICE

CHRISTINA:
How Pathetic I Am!

Shadow, shadow on the wall,
Who is the most pathetic of all?

KOAN

When Christina joined a group of longtime meditators, she asked, "Why don't we share our practice by taking turns giving short Dharma talks?"

The group members became upset. "We can give instruction about posture and breathing," they said, "but we need to have a proper teacher, at least a monk, to give a Dharma talk. We householders cannot do that under any circumstances."

Christina felt a chill in her heart. She thought, am I also afraid of owning my practice in this way? If so, how pathetic I am!

REFLECTION

Only you can live in your own skin and stand on your own feet. Whose guidance do you need to confirm this fact? When the group members became upset at Christina's suggestion, she saw that hidden behind the façade of a healthy respect for tradition, there was a subtle fear that mirrored something very deep in herself. One of Christina's struggles was her difficulty, even strong resistance to, owning that she, just as she is, is a complete and perfect expression of the life force. She felt that the good little girl who was always seeking for someone's approval and sanctioning was alive in her despite her age and decades of Buddhist practice. Realizing this, she declared to herself: *How pathetic that I am like this! How pathetic that after all these years of practice, I am still unwilling to completely own who I am!*

Is this true of you, too? How pathetic are you?

The great challenge of spiritual life is that no one can realize for you who you truly are. As the Zen Master Kodo Sasaki said, "You can't trade even a single fart with the next guy. Each and every one of us has to live out his own life."[55] Who you are is not dependent on whether someone approves or disapproves, affirms or denies, gives or takes away anything from you. No one can live your life for you—you must stand fully on your own ground. You cannot live someone else's life—to try to do so is to negate the truth of that person. You are unique, a complete manifestation of the universal life force; the other person is so, too.

It is not uncommon for people to feel that someone wearing a robe or using a title is somehow superior, knows more, or is more important than they are. A worthy teacher will flip all your assumptions and throw them back at you for examination. You will probably not like this much because your sense of inadequacy and unworthiness may be triggered. Or you may simply be perplexed, as when Zen Master Huangbo called his students *gobblers of dregs* and demanded, "Don't you know that there are no Zen teachers in all of China?" "And what about you?" a student asked. Huangbo prodded, "I don't say there is no Zen, only that there are no teachers."[56] This does not mean that companions of the Way are not a treasure, or that a teacher is not a treasure.

Unwittingly, Christina had challenged the group. Zen talks are meant to shake you out of your sense of yourself, not make you feel good about yourself. Sometimes a simple question can rattle foundations. Christina's suggestion had that impact, exposing a group taboo. Groups have shadows just as individuals do, with certain subjects that are never discussed or examined in order not to upset the status quo. It takes strong intentionality and commitment for a person or group to identify and examine these taboos.

You can easily overlook how group members can act as guides and teachers, including yourself. Playing such a role demands taking full responsibility for your own practice and for the group's practice. It means dropping judgments about each other, revealing aspects of yourself, and respecting the interdependence and wisdom that are inherent in each person. The Dharma can be taught in an empowering way when group members hold practice circles and discussions, witnessing each other's journey.

Can a group of spiritual practitioners challenge themselves to awaken together? Can you be a true spiritual friend in this way? Without a teacher, how do you know when you're starting to go off the rails? How do you know when you're just stagnating as a group of practitioners? Awakening together invites all members of the group to question everything in each other's company, including the foundations of the group itself.

When you can throw out your assumptions and begin anew each moment with respect and equanimity, you will not be pathetic.

———

When do you stop needing external approval and trust that you are the complete manifestation of Life itself? Can you confidently exchange practice and support with your fellow practitioners? What changes do you and your group need to make to facilitate this?

JEFFREY:
Dr. Doctor Rides the Bus

Depending on circumstances,
Everything is medicine,
Everything is disease.
Doctors are no exception.

KOAN

Dr. Doctor had a common cold, but he still rode the bus to work. He began to cough and sneeze into his handkerchief. Every time he coughed, all the people on the bus tried to cough. Every time he sneezed, all the people on the bus tried to sneeze. Finally, the doctor exited at his destination.

"Whew!" the driver sighed. "What would we do without good medical advice?"

REFLECTION

Ah, the voice of authority! When the good doctor is in, some of us feel free to leave our mind outside the waiting room. We listen to her, imitate her, copy her mannerisms, walk like her, and sit like her, thinking it will lead to the same results. But not only are we different from each other, we're also changing all the time. How do we know what to do at this moment?

We get so much advice in this digital age. We can access articles on vitamins, health, diet, exercise, and how to eliminate wrinkles. We get links to videos and clips on the merits of meditation, the practice of gratitude, the discipline of mindfulness, and the importance of wisdom and compassion. With all this free advice running about, with all this complex knowledge available to us with a click of a mouse, why do we still catch colds? Why are we more obese and stressed than before? With connection to gurus, experts, and TED talks, why do we so often feel hollow, cynical, and disconnected?

Once I spoke on the phone with a friend who was coming down to San Francisco after completing a long, expensive course of study. Driving down Highway 101 towards the Golden Gate Bridge, he was on top of the world. He loved his teachers, he had great openings, and life was transformed. But soon I could hear him muttering under his breath about the traffic backed up before the bridge. Some minutes passed, and I could hear him getting angrier and angrier, until finally I heard him yell at somebody. What happened, I asked. "F—ing guy at the toll-booth told me to stop because the cars aren't moving on the bridge! What stupid a—holes, doesn't anybody know what to do here?"

Your teachers usually loom large in your mind. They've given you so much, maybe lighting a beacon through some very dark places. At the same time, the practice for healing the planet and ourselves isn't automatically sneezing and coughing like them.

How do you take responsibility for your life? Eat what's on your plate right now. Do what's in front of you at this moment. Be a responsible human being in your interactions with spouse or partner, your child, parents, a co-worker, the telemarketer who calls inopportunely on the phone, the cashier at the bank, the dog that gets into the compost pile.

You may not have a title or position, but don't you have the power to decide and take action in your own life? If you're not that authority, who is? A doctor, a teacher, a parent, an employer, a guru, God? When it's one of these, the end is often cynicism, a rejection of all authority, refusing to acknowledge anyone as a teacher or guide, recognizing no value in his/her teachings or advice.

There's the famous story of Nan-in, the nineteenth-century Zen master who was asked by a professor for teachings on Zen. He served his guest tea, and kept on pouring even after the cup was full and the tea spilled out. When asked what he was doing, Nan-in said, "How can I teach you anything if your mind is full of your own opinions and ideas? If you want to learn something, first empty your mind."[57]

Empty your mind of blind awe and mechanical obedience, as well as of distrust and cynicism, listen deeply, and take action. Your life is your own. Taizan Maezumi told his American successors: *Take as much of this as you can. Swallow what you need and spit out the rest.*[58]

Imitating anyone, no matter how credentialed or exalted, leads to everyone getting a cold.

———

"If your teacher tells you to jump off the roof, you must do so,"
said a visiting Japanese teacher to an American sangha in the early
1980s. If you had heard these words, what would you have done?
Who is your voice of authority?

ARIEL:

Modern Nirvana

Da dailytwitamin ICYMI
ILUVU 4EVA&EVA CU L8R
XOXOXOXOXOXOXOXOXOXO
Tell me, what mishigas lol is this?

KOAN

A skeptical student asked a teacher, "Is it still possible to attain Nirvana in this modern age?"

REFLECTION

If you are enlightened to the truth of this koan, you can see your web traffic skyrocket and plummet, add two million followers, tweet nonstop, and add your personal signature to one million documents without running out of ink or tiring your hand.

Wow, that's a lot of activity! What happens to your attention when you feel overwhelmed by YouTubes and emails, the requests to be someone's *Friend* or *Fan*, to *Link*, *Like*, *Tweet*, or *Share*, and wish happy birthday to a million people every day?

According to the sutras, when the Buddha sat under the Bodhi tree, the tempter Mara threw delusion after delusion at him, everything from horrifying demons to Mara's own gorgeous daughters, to distract, seduce, or frighten him. Our present-day Mara provides glaring headlines about the economy, hate messages on social media, viral videos, and online porn sites. It sells retirement packages, sexy negligees, advanced university degrees, and dharma webinars about how to become enlightened.

What do we do with such information overload? How do we awaken?

We are more connected than ever before to far-flung nations, reading avidly about cultures and societies very different from our own and of which we were mostly ignorant until only several decades ago. We follow the destruction of hurricanes and earthquakes as they happen half a world away, spaceships hurtling through space, and the latest medical research done in a distant laboratory. We get summoned electronically to political rallies, reminded that it's time to refill our prescriptions, invited to play games and message the world, and warned of the end of life as we know it on a specific date.

What do we stand on? How do we decide when to say yes and when to say no? What happens to our vows? Bombarded by unending pleas, requests, and invitations, do we sometimes feel our stability slipping away? What do we do with the anxiety and fear that arise in the midst of all this speed and instant accessibility?

Perhaps most important, what do we do with our attention? When I'm reading an article online, am I actually reading it or skimming through it in order to get to the next article? Am I giving things my conscious attention, or mostly checking things off? Am I living my life or taking an inventory of it?

Zen meditation asks us to bring our attention back to the breath, or the koan, or to *Now*, each time it wanders. It is a slow and meticulous practice, but over time we begin to experience the settling of both body and mind. How do you remain settled throughout the day even as phones, emails, texts, and various apps clamor for your attention?

Eihei Dogen wrote: "[The Whole Body] is never apart from one right where one is."[59] Wherever you are—on your cushion, in your desk chair or car seat, or even on your feet while standing at the oven cooking dinner—the whole world is right there doing those things. How do you experience that? By practicing it. By living it. Is there really any reason to look right or left, to run to the phone or the computer screen, to fragment your awareness, and give away that priceless commodity of attention for information bytes that are no sooner read than forgotten? Says Dogen: "If you concentrate your effort single-mindedly, that in itself is negotiating the Way."

A student said to Master Ichu, "Please write for me something of great wisdom."

Master Ichu picked up his brush and wrote one word: "Attention."

The student said, "Is that all?"

The master wrote, "Attention. Attention."

The student became irritable. "That doesn't seem profound or subtle to me."

In response, Master Ichu wrote simply, "Attention. Attention. Attention."

In frustration, the student demanded, "What does this word attention mean?"

Master Ichu replied, "Attention means attention."[60]

Master Ichu knew this secret before Facebook, before Twitter and Instagram, before modern-day treasure hunters began to relentlessly seek attention. Your attention. Where will you give it?

We can also consciously decide not to pay attention for a while, not to focus on anything in particular. For example, meandering, or goalless walking, does not aim towards a destination or result; it's simply rambling about, looking around, giving yourself permission to pay attention to what you pass on the road, or not. Effortlessly, you become more attuned to your body and the world around you; you notice clouds, sun, and clouds again, and enjoy the ease of a lazy afternoon.

Would you call spending time in this way a waste of a day?

Whatever activity—or inactivity—you engage in, do it wholeheartedly. Give yourself to your life fully. Not half a self, not while texting or watching YouTube. Don't cut your heart in half or quarters, keep it whole, fully here now.

———

Can you carve out times during the day when you're just doing one thing completely? Can you give full attention to the task in front of you? The food in front of you? How about to the person in front of you?

—

SHISHIN:
Golden Buddha

—

When you meet the Buddha,
How will you greet him?
If you say a word, he can't hear you.
If you keep silent, he won't know you are here.
Tell me: What will you do?

KOAN

One night, Shishin had a dream. He and his teacher were sitting in the meditation hall when a brilliant golden light shone suddenly from a corner of the room.

Shishin whispered to his teacher, "The Buddha is here."

His teacher smiled and said, "Yes! Let's go and greet the Buddha."

Shishin did not hesitate. He got up from his seat and walked over to the light, which was so bright that he couldn't look directly at it. Lowering his entire body to the floor, he bowed reverently. Prostrated, he felt the warm light wash all over him and a deep sense of peace welled up inside.

Later, his teacher asked, "What did the Buddha give you that was not already yours?"

REFLECTION

Shishin sat zazen for years, even hosting a sitting group and organizing retreats, all the while supporting his family and raising his children. Throughout it all, he experienced a profound dis-ease and felt inadequate as a Zen practitioner.

In particular, Shishin was frustrated with his lack of an experience of enlightenment. Having come of age at a time when enlightenment experiences were the gold standard of American Zen practice, he desired an experience so transformative that he would never feel unworthy or have a sense of dis-ease ever again.

Settling into the practice of sitting, Shishin realized that one persistent thought came up early each morning: *I am not good enough*. This life-denying mantra was the background music to his life, a tightly woven narrative against which he measured himself, an ever-present destructive and traumatizing voice. The more Shishin meditated, the more overwhelmed he felt by this voice. But tell me, did Shishin fundamentally lack anything to begin with?

Do you believe that transcendent experiences will eliminate these debilitating voices? In my own practice, awareness of *I am not enough* led me to a sad inner child that called out for my attention. I learned to ask her what was wrong and what was it that she needed. I allowed myself to experience her sadness and to give her what she needed. What is your inner child asking of you today? Listen carefully, experience the feelings, and tend to them. In this way, you can take care of the persistent voice within.

What beliefs do you harbor about yourself? Do these beliefs take the form of negative thoughts that are not spoken out loud but with which you are in constant conversation inside? And do you measure yourself against them without ever questioning their validity? Is your self-narrative true? How do you know?

In the midst of the rough and tumble of his daily life, Shishin clung to a regular sitting practice. Sitting was what he knew to do, and he did it. The Zen Master Kodo Sawaki said, "Zazen is good for nothing." Just sit. This is a strong prescription when the mind is overrun with debilitating thoughts of unworthiness; it is an even stronger medicine when there is no promise or sign of anything changing. What are your reasons for doing your spiritual practice? What do you want to happen? It's best to be honest with yourself about your expectations.

In his dream, Shishin whispered, "The Buddha is here." Where is *here*? In the meditation room? In the bathroom? On the street? Everywhere! There is nowhere that the Buddha's light does not permeate. The light from the Buddha was so bright that Shishin could not look at it, yet he did not hesitate when his teacher said, "Let's go say hello!" What a daring invitation! The Buddha is right here, now. How will you greet the Buddha?

Who is Buddha? Can you tap your very own body and say, "This?" Over time we realize that Buddha is nothing but our own body. Conditioned as we are to seek outside of ourselves, we are perplexed: How can I possibly be Buddha?

When he prostrated reverently on the floor, Shishin felt the warm bright light and profound sense of peace wash over himself from the bottom of his feet to the top of his head. When prostrating, we lower our self-centeredness to the ground and lift the Buddha's heart-mind above our heads. Many years ago, in my

THE BOOK OF HOUSEHOLDER KOANS

own practice, I bowed alone all night long while chanting softly with each bow, "Being one with Great Compassion Avalokitesvara Bodhisattva." Suddenly, the Bodhisattva herself appeared before me. The next morning, my teacher, sensing that something was different, asked, "What happened to you?" When I told him, he said, "I told you: When you call the bodhisattvas, they will come!"

Through all the years of meditation, Shishin, by taking the posture of Shakyamuni Buddha in the midst of his own dis-ease, had been calling to the Buddha. One night, the gap between Shishin and the Buddha closed. When Shishin awoke from his dream, he rose from his bed and sat in a cross-legged meditation posture. His whole being was suffused with the extraordinary vivid peace of the Buddha.

Later, his teacher asked him, "What did the Buddha give you that was not already yours?"

Bring the Buddha to me right now!

———

Identify a belief about yourself. Investigate it! What beliefs do you harbor about your spiritual practice? Investigate them! What is your inner child asking of you? Provide it! What is Buddha doing right now?

MYONEN:
White Wolf

A wolf in grandma's clothing:
Big eyes, tall ears, sharp teeth—
And a traveler with a red hood.
What a bloody mess when they meet!

KOAN

Bill saw Myonen going into the woods with her dogs. "Where are you going?" he asked.

"To see the white wolf inside the forest."

"Don't be silly, everyone knows there are no wolves in Massachusetts," said Bill. "Beside, white wolves are only in the Arctic."

Myonen entered the forest.

REFLECTION

A long time ago, sitting on a rock by pools deep in a state-owned forest, Myonen looked out beyond the trees to a clearing far away and saw a large white animal. In all the years that she'd been visiting that spot she'd seen deer, coyotes, and bears, but nothing white, not even a dog. She thought it might be a white wolf, and every day thereafter, for years, she'd look out towards that distant clearing seeking it.

Aren't the great stories of our lives searches, journeys, and quests? Whether it's revelation, a holy grail, a snow leopard, an odyssey, enlightenment, or going home, these tales are archetypal for most cultures and peoples. Even if we don't have a grand plan or lofty ambitions, chances are we still see our life's arc as some kind of quest or journey of discovery.

And doesn't every quest and journey need help? Not just help from the rational mind, but also from the irrational, the things that make no sense. Day by day the curtain comes up briefly to reveal such glimpses. What are those, if not marvelous aspects of ourselves? Magic happens, coincidences occur, strangers make uncanny remarks, sudden bursts of memory come seemingly out of nowhere. A stranger emails from halfway around the world with an idea, an offer of help. A deer appears in the woods, veers, and runs right towards me just as I'm pondering a retreat with Lakota elders in their sacred Black Hills.

Since we're not separate from the universe, there's no such thing as a call without response, but the response is in the universe's language, or languages. Can you listen? How attached are you to daily routines keeping you from looking right or left? How attached are you to your rational mind? There is nothing wrong with our rational mind, but when we rely on it excessively, don't we leave out the irrational, the intuitive, the imaginary? Don't we leave out the white wolf in the forest?

Master Jizo asked Hogen, "Where have you come from?"
"I pilgrimage aimlessly," replied Hogen.
"What is the matter of your pilgrimage?" asked Jizo.
"I don't know," replied Hogen.
"Not knowing is the most intimate," replied Jizo.[61]

Jizo's asking: When you embark on a quest or journey, what are you searching for? Is it anything that can be defined or described by your logical brain? Is it anything that makes sense?

Mystery is the provenance of nature, so it's no wonder that so many meditators go to do retreats in mountain monasteries or forest refuges. But everything can be rolled into your practice, from an old melody you can't get out of your head to a haunting memory that won't let go. Without meandering in accordance with the wishes of our heart, practice can become dry and rational, or else too rarefied, because it doesn't include the full human being. It doesn't mean we have to give up our householder life of family and work. In the midst of a busy life, we can still pilgrimage aimlessly.

Did Myonen ever see another white wolf in the woods of Massachusetts? Was it a delusion? A dream? A disappointed goal? Does it matter? Instead, she pays attention to daily changes, to how trees come down after storms, their branches carted off by the stream, ducks landing in the pools, coyote scat on the trail. Doing this day after day for years, she no longer even notices when she enters or leaves the forest. In the winter, with the ground buried under snow, she walks only a short way in, looks up at the tall pines and down below at the frozen creek, and turns back. Those few footsteps are all that's needed. The hoot of an owl is all that's needed; the slow, winding fall of a maple leaf long past its prime is all that's needed.

Since each step is a destination, why go far?

———

Is there something in your life that appears and reappears, and won't let go? How do you follow it?

BUTSUGEN:

My Tongue Is Tied

When inner turmoil overcomes you,
What's to be done?
When your tongue is tied,
Speak! Speak!

KOAN

Butsugen yearned to become sober so he began attending meetings of Alcoholics Anonymous several times a day. He was told that it was very important to share at the meetings, but he was in a state of such intense inner turmoil that he could not say a word. He tried to speak, but no words came. One night when Butsugen felt that he was truly at the end of his rope, a woman shared, saying words that expressed his own distress and anguish.

In the midst of his anguish, Butsugen smiled.

REFLECTION

Why did Butsugen smile?

Do you know this condition when you must speak but no words come? Staying silent is too painful, yet the voice is paralyzed. It is like the story of a man hanging from a tree branch by his mouth: His hands can't grasp a bough, his feet can't touch the ground. A stranger stands below and shouts, "What is the meaning of your life?"[62] Or, "What are you really doing at the AA meeting, Butsugen?"

Butsugen yearned for a life beyond his addiction. He attended the AA meetings again and again, each time feeling even more vulnerable. His discomfort was intense and yet he felt powerless to do anything about it. He could not give up on the meetings and yet he could not untie his tongue to speak—he was dangling at the end of his rope, like the person in the tree.

How will you save yourself? Whatever the addiction—alcohol, tobacco, sugar, drugs, or sex—it takes courage to face the deep yearning to find fulfillment in the fullness of your being.

A Zen teacher said, "We are all addicted to the self." So how about the addiction to the ego-centered self? Is clinging to self-centeredness and the unrelenting suffering that ensues an addiction common to everyone? Even if you're not addicted to a substance, do you cling to a sense of a solid, fixed, permanent self that becomes your reference point for everything you think and do? How will you save yourself from that?

Self-centeredness is so ingrained that, like the person up in the tree, it's hard to even consider letting go. You think that holding on will save you or that letting go will kill you. But tell me, *who* is holding on to *what*? As you become even more aware of what exactly *you* are clinging to, the problem may appear worse than ever! Rest assured, however, that a growing awareness and attention to clinging are big steps toward being free.

The immediate relief for Butsugen came in the form of a woman sharing her own anguish, using the very words he himself would have used had he been able to untie his tongue. When you recognize yourself in another, you expand beyond your limitations. "It is like she was living inside me," Butsugen said. In an instant, he recognized himself and felt recognized, too. He still had to do the challenging inner work needed for sobriety, but when he was at his most vulnerable, another person's words helped him to stay sober for one more day. Truly, there was a lot for Butsugen to smile about. But can you tell me why he smiled?

The journey to sobriety is best undertaken in the company of other like-hearted people. It is a rare gift to meet a healing community. Seeing yourself in others can be profoundly healing. In this way, the Buddhist sangha can fulfill the same function for our addictions to the self as an AA group does for alcoholism. Some Zen communities focus so exclusively on meditation and silence that they barely speak to one another. Once a friend was invited to speak at a Zen group. Noticing that the person who had invited her was not there, she inquired about him by name. No one knew who he was. Perplexed, she described the blue truck that he drove and, at last, everyone said, "Oh, yes, we know the guy who drives the blue truck!"

Many sanghas today, however, have processes like councils, circles, and other such practices that encourage listening and sharing to help you recognize yourself. Butsugen never got to tell the woman how she had saved him that evening. He now takes comfort in the understanding that he too, just by showing up for his life every day, may actually be saving someone else.

How are you showing up?

Speak quickly, speak quickly!

When your tongue is tied, how will you find the way through? Tell me of a moment when you recognized yourself in someone else.

Kit's New Practice

Where on the compass do you find being human?
North South East West.
Look up, then down.
Or just Google.

KOAN

Kit asked the teacher: "What practice should I follow now?"

"Pretend to be human," answered the teacher.

"But I am human!" protested Kit.

"That is why you must pretend," replied the teacher.

REFLECTION

A friend's five-year-old crawled on her knees: "Ruff! Ruff!"

I asked her what she was doing.

"I'm pretending."

"Are you pretending that you're a cat?"

"No, silly, I'm pretending to be a dog."

"How are you doing that?"

"Ruff! Ruff!"

I liked the game so much that the next day I pretended to be a human. I got up in the morning and took a shower. I made myself some coffee and did meditation. I said good morning to my husband and fed the dog.

What do we humans mean when we say we're human? A cat goes *meow*, a dog goes *ruff*, a cow goes *moo*, and a human goes—what? A kangaroo hops, a hawk flies, a snake slithers, a flower blooms, and a human—? Is there any one thing that makes us human?

Back in the seventeenth century, Descartes thought that thinking is what makes us human. Since then, scientists have tried to identify other traits that make us different from other species, like language, altruism, and the ability to make tools, but research shows that things we once thought were exclusive to us are also shared by other species. Life forms, with all their variations, seem to be much more fluid than anyone thought.

Is it true that all hawks fly and all flowers bloom? And if the would-be hawks are still fledglings and the rose petals don't bloom, are they not hawks or flowers?

What makes anything what it is? When I say this is a candle, this is grass, this is a lawn chair, this is a man, this is a woman, I'm pointing to certain aspects that in my mind characterize a candle, grass, a lawn chair, and all the rest. A candle burns, grass is green, and a lawn chair sits on a lawn. But if these comprised their basic essence, wouldn't that essence remain the same under any condition? And yet we could think of conditions—a hurricane, a frost—that extinguish candles, cause the grass to go brown, and let fly or destroy the lawn chair.

My teacher likes to say: Just be a human being, that's the best practice. But what is the essence of a human being? Maybe the essence of being a human being is seeing that there is no one identifiable essence.

Many years ago my teacher and I walked together in Birkenau, part of the Auschwitz-Birkenau concentration camp compound. There, passing along crumbling barracks and the remains of gas chambers and crematoria, he said: "We want so much to believe that there's something that's common to everyone. Philosophers and religious leaders all try to find and point to it: What's that basic thing? The only thing that I can see we all have in common is our differences."

We have fought wars over questions like what constitutes a real human being. Witness the rage around the issue of abortion, look at what has transpired in this country in the name of race! Can we even agree on what it is to be a male or a female? We used to think it was all about biology, but more and more people now claim a gender identification that is more fluid, based on feeling rather than on the body they were born to. We can't even agree on the essence of good food or good music.

Is there any reason we should agree? When we say that everything is interdependent, we mean it's all relational, contextual, conditioned on circumstances. So what absolute truth are we fighting about? Why do we subscribe to ideas like *the real deal, the real stuff*? Is everything else less real?

Even as I say *that's who I really am*, or *that's the real me*, boundless molecules and cells in my body are assembling and disassembling at incalculable speeds, changing me so quickly my consciousness can never keep up.

Given that, is there anything we can do other than pretend?

235

———

What's the real you? Is there one thing you can point to with total certainty?

KODO:

Solitary Angler

Look! Look!
What do you see when there is Nothing to see?
An ancient fisherman hooks a suburban housewife.

KOAN

One day as she was relaxing in her favorite chair, Kodo flipped through a book and came upon Ma Yuan's thirteenth-century Chinese painting titled *The Solitary Angler*. In the painting, a lone fisherman sits at the bow of a wooden boat in the middle of a vast lake, his fishing line dangling over the side of the boat.

Kodo cried out, "That's me! That's me as I truly am, but I am not yet that. How do I become *that*?"

REFLECTION

Who are you? My teacher, Maezumi Roshi, often instructed us to close the gap between who you think you are and who you truly are. "Close the gap," he would say, "between the Self and your-self." The Self is unconditional, so how do you close the gap so that there is no sense of separation, no sense of *you* or *me?*

When Kodo saw Ma Yuan's painting, it cut through to her very essence. How is it that an African-American woman in New Jersey was called forth by a painting of an ancient Chinese fish-erman? The essence of life, the original nature itself as captured by the artist Ma Yuan, resonated throughout her body. It didn't matter that the painting was of a different century, an unknown place, and an unfamiliar culture, nothing that resembled Kodo or her life.

What pierced through all the layers of time, place, and person?

What awakened in Kodo?

Ma Yuan's painting exudes stillness and silence, a sense of infinite vastness. A humble fisherman appears in this vastness; he is neither separate from it nor other than it. He is woven of the same nature as the fishing line, the water, the entire universe itself. Seeing this, Kodo felt a stirring deep within. She sensed immedi-ately that there was something for her to uncover about her own being that Ma Yuan had captured. From this moment on, the urge to know *that* consumed Kodo's life.

What is this shift that Kodo experienced? Do you recall the moment when you felt the pull towards something beyond the conventional and material, beyond the division of *you* and *me?* It's a shift away from a self-centered way of living in which your ideas and desires form the basis for everything. Once you glimpse something beyond *you* and *me*, you can never be fully satisfied. The urge to affirm experientially the essential nature of life is a powerful force. This was Kodo's question: How could she expe-rience herself *as-is?*

Who is searching for what? At the outset of the spiritual journey as depicted in *The Ten Oxherding Pictures*, a verse says, "Till now, the ox has never been lost."[63] The great Chinese ancestor Ma Tsu said, "*That* which asks the question is your treasure house. It contains absolutely everything you need and lacks nothing at all. It is there for you to use freely, so why this vain search for something outside of yourself?"[64] What is this vast treasure house that you are? The ancients say that it is beyond thinking. Ma Tsu says that it contains everything. What is it?

The *Heart Sutra* expounds this in the famous words: *Form is emptiness and emptiness is form.* How can you know the unconditioned, that which is fundamentally without dualisms like you and me, right and wrong, good and bad? Just as the painting awakened the treasure in Kodo, you, too, are called to know yourself at this deepest possible level. Zen masters say, "You don't sit in zazen in order to become a Buddha. You sit because you are a Buddha to begin with." Your treasure house is waiting to be uncovered, opened, and used freely. So, tell me, how will you know it?

I meditated for the first time many years ago in a seven-day Zen sesshin. During the sesshin, something awakened so powerfully inside that I just had to follow where it took me. At the time, I knew nothing about spiritual practice or realizing one's true nature, had never heard the phrase *Buddha recognizes Buddha, and Buddha calls to Buddha,* had in fact no words for my experience. I left my marriage, my work, and the city where I lived, and followed whatever that was that needed to know itself. When *Buddha calls to Buddha,* there is no stopping this powerful movement within. There is no right or wrong way to do this—you might remain at home as Kodo did, you might leave home as I did, or some combination of the two. Frankly, you just don't know where the urge to realize your true self will lead you.

A thirteenth-century Chinese fisherman called out to a contemporary African-American housewife; the Buddha's posture of crossed-legged sitting called out to me. What is calling you forth? Your essential nature is continually calling you home. Chances are if you are reading this, you are already responding to the call. When you return home to yourself, you realize that you have always been home, dwelling just as you are in *that* as *that,* the treasure house itself. The utterly unique being that you are is the perfect expression of *that*; the hands holding this book and eyes scanning the page are the perfect harmony of form and emptiness, complete and whole, lacking nothing, and cannot and need not be otherwise.

———

Show me yourself as the treasure house. When your treasure house opens, how will you use it? Where is Ma Yuan's fisherman now?

Dantika's Dream

Gott, Gut, Gutt, Good, God.
What's in a name?
What will you do when words fail you
And no sound comes?

KOAN

Dantika had a dream:

On the first morning of retreat, she is told to sit on the zendo monitor's cushion. To her surprise, she finds two bells—one the usual zendo monitor's bell, a second smaller one—and only one striker. She rings the usual bell three times to begin the first meditation period, but she hears no sound. She tries again, then decides to ring the smaller bell. No sound comes out of that bell, either. Feeling rushed and frustrated, she hits the bell with such force that the striker breaks.

She shows the broken striker to the senior student next to her, asking for direction.

Gutt says, "Just begin."

REFLECTION

Who or what is *Gutt*? Is it the senior student? Does it refer to God, which is *Gott* in German?

Or is it Dantika's *gut*?

The zendo monitor's practice is to prepare the zendo for meditation and to signal the beginning and end of sitting periods by hitting the bell. In meditation centers we train people to take care of the meditation space. They come in early, put on the heat, set up the cushions, and when everyone is seated they hit the bell. Only this time no sound came.

Dantika tries a second time, and still there is no sound. So she hits the bell with such force that the striker breaks.

Can we relate to such a situation? We do our best and abide by the rules, and things don't turn out. We get fired from our job, our marriage ends, our children grow up differently from what we expected. Over and over, life takes a path that unsettles us. Craters appear in the asphalt of the road, accidents, detours, construction, destruction, even complete closures, and still we're surprised. *It's not supposed to be this way!* As soon as we deal with one thing, something new turns up: a bell that doesn't ring, a striker that breaks, a car that won't start, a leak in the roof.

Every one of these events is an opportunity to experience the vitality and unpredictability of this moment. We meditate regularly to realize this, sometimes depending too much on quiet and a lack of disruption. It's often the "mishaps" that wake us out of the stupor we call routine. Do we see it as an invitation to have an adventure, try a new approach, do something new, or do we get frustrated and self-conscious about making mistakes?

When the latter happens, you could look to your teacher or a senior student for instruction. You could also listen to "Gutt," or gut, when it tells you to just begin.

How do you begin when the bell doesn't ring?

Make it up. Get creative. Sing aloud the ringing of the bell. Clap your hands or hit the floor three times. Just begin.

One day, Yen Kuan called to his attendant, "Bring me my rhinoceros-horn fan."

The attendant said, "The fan is broken."

Yen Kuan said, "If the fan is broken, bring the rhinoceros back to me."[65]

Every moment demands of us to present our mind, spontaneous, dynamic, untethered to patterns of the past. Can we improvise, think out of the box? Come up with a new sound or a new food dish? Come up with a rhinoceros?

"It Don't Mean a Thing (If It Ain't Got That Swing)," wrote Duke Ellington. Doesn't every situation call for its own "swing," its own freshness of response? The broken fan, the bell that won't ring, the broken striker—this is us. We're all in this together. There are days when we are broken, when we can't ring, when we don't say and do what is usual and expected. For some of us, those are the days we can't get out of bed. For others, those are the days when we fly.

Since we're shattered anyway, why not start from scratch? Why not try out a new song, go to work by a different road, get down and dirty in the sandbox with your little child, or get into a long conversation with a street person you've seen many times and always ignored?

"The rhinoceros-horn fan has long been in use," says the verse on the koan. "In summer, cool, in winter, warm. Everyone has it, why don't they know?" There is a fan to cool us in summer and warm us in winter, we all have it. That same fan can provide cool air when it's warm and it can also circulate heat when it's cold. So, tell me, how do you fan yourself? What does Gutt say?

———

In what situations do you feel self-conscious and afraid of making mistakes? What's the worst that can happen? If the worst happens, what will you do?

Penelope Tells the Truth

Tell the whole truth.
Tell nothing but the truth.
What's the truth?
Tell me, what do you know?

KOAN

Penelope's chaplaincy supervisor had an alcoholic husband. After a particularly uncomfortable public event at which the husband was drunk, Penelope spoke to her supervisor about how this situation affected the chaplaincy program. The supervisor received Penelope's truth-telling with an icy cold stare. Penelope's life in the chaplaincy program became very difficult after that and she was eventually transferred to another hospital.

Penelope told her teacher what happened. The teacher listened intently for a long time and then asked her, "What would have happened if you had not spoken?"

Penelope was struck dumb.

REFLECTION

Do you tell the truth, the whole truth, and nothing but the truth?

From the time she was a little girl, Penelope took on the mantle of family "truth teller," the one who spoke up when no one else would. In a group of friends, at school, and later at work, she assumed the role of the one who named the "truth" that others felt and did not say aloud. Sometimes there were rewards and sometimes not. This became a strong, ingrained habit.

So when Penelope's teacher asked her, "What would have happened if you had not spoken?" Penelope was struck dumb by the question. She could not speak or think. The question was like an arrow shot at her most basic identity: She was the truth teller, the one who could be counted upon to speak the truth regardless of consequences. It was an unexamined pattern of behavior that had long defined who she was.

Tell me, do you, too, slip into a particular pattern of behavior, an unexamined, habitual rut? What self-identity have you not examined?

Are you a truth teller or are you someone who avoids telling the truth? What is truth? My teacher, Bernie Glassman, would say that there are all kinds of truths: factual, mythological, emotional, scientific, psychological, and spiritual truths. How do you know that something is *the truth*? Or, is it, as Bernie later came to say, just your opinion?

Sometimes a simple question hits its target, freeing you from deeply held assumptions you hold about yourself. You can identify these assumptions by listening to your own internal voice, such as when it keeps repeating, "I am the only one who speaks the truth about such and such." What happens when actions you consider so right, even heroic, trigger a most unwelcome reaction from others? You might be defensive and self-righteous even in the face of dire consequences, all under the guise of caring about others. How do you move out of your own conditioned patterns into a more open, unconditioned view?

In Zen practice, we learn to pause and consider the context—the time, place, person, and amount of response—before speaking and acting. Although the old wiring to speak out may still surge, you will develop the capacity to say *Wait!* and discern if speech is needed and, if so, what kind of speech is best. You can ask yourself: "Am I trying to manipulate the situation and shape how I want it to be?" When your wish to change a situation or person arises, are you serving the whole situation or just your motives?

Even as you learn to be more skillful in your everyday actions and speech, don't settle for that. Keep raising the question: *What is this?* Try plunging into someone else's world and bear witness to their reality without imposing your judgments and points of view. When your point of view dominates, you cannot see the actual situation. In the realm of the bodhisattvas, the great beings of compassion and wisdom, you are always aiming to end or minimize suffering. You can only do this when you clearly see the circumstances and context in which you are functioning. There is no room for self-serving motivations.

Wherever you find yourself, can you let your egotistical interest shatter? Don't be fooled by yourself!

———

How do you investigate someone else's truth? How does that change your perception of what is true?

GYOKUUN:
Genetically Modified

So, what's all the fuss about?
Sitting and retreating,
Saying no, saying yes,
Birth and death
Nothing but deluded bookends.
The smoke of sandalwood disappears,
Leaving a pungent smell.

KOAN

Gyokuun asked: "How many genes does it take to make a Buddha?"
    Someone replied: "One more, one less."

REFLECTION

During his enlightenment experience, the Buddha said that he and the entire world are enlightened. Doesn't that include us? We're all Buddhas, all awakened beings, only we don't know it. Why?

Maybe because we've been genetically modified. Our individual strands of DNA and our different histories and cultures not only make us different from Shakyamuni Buddha and the great Zen masters of China and Japan, but also from Zen masters in the West, and also from each other.

Nevertheless, we're all enlightened as we are.

We have a beautiful, wooden, many-armed Kwan Yin, the Bodhisattva of Compassion, on an altar in our living room. Over many years and numerous moves, she's lost some of the arms she depends on to take care of the world. In addition, her torso has broken into three separate pieces that have been glued together several times. Is she any less a Buddha for all that?

Or how about my own Buddha, standing on the altar in my office, having lost one of his feet so that he seems to be balancing on one leg? Or my husband after his stroke? Or the homeless woman talking to herself on the pavement outside? Or the bully sending hate messages on Facebook? How about the killer serving time on death row for murdering a child?

The Zen Peacemakers have done annual retreats at Auschwitz-Birkenau for close to twenty years. Always we have chanted the names of those who died there. One year someone proposed also chanting the names of Nazi perpetrators, and we had a near riot.

How many genes does it take to make a Buddha? What does it take to misplace your Buddha nature—the loss of a hand, a foot, a mind? The loss of kindness, caring, a heart? Can you ever really lose your Buddha nature?

We're genetically modified, different from each other, and whole and complete as we are. The Buddha knew it; we don't, so we scramble this way and that, trying to find our way, trying to find ourselves.

In his poem "The Sycamore,"[66] Wendell Berry writes of the tree:

"Fences have been tied to it, nails driven into it,
    hacks and whittles cut in it, the lightning has burned it.
    There is no year it has flourished in
    That has not harmed it."

And then he adds:

". . . It has risen to a strange perfection
    in the warp and bending of its long growth."

Don't we all warp and bend even as we try to be better husbands, wives, parents, and children? Reaching out towards others, we stretch so hard that at times we can't recognize our own contours and proportions.

Where do we feel most settled? At home. Where is that? "Home is within you, or home is nowhere at all," wrote Herman Hesse. We can carry home with us wherever we go because it's not a particular place, a special room, or a corner by a fireplace. We're whole as we are, enlightened as we are.

How do we experience this? By living it. Not only am I enlightened as I am, so is this cup of coffee, so is my child running upstairs to tell me about her day in school, so is my mother calling me on the telephone from far away. Buddha Nature manifesting as all beings, sentient and insentient.

Recognizing this, how am I living my life?

———

Do you experience edges in your life, personal qualities and situations you're not comfortable with? Which of these disqualifies you from being a Buddha?

CHOSUI:
Old Bear

*"A wiser fella once said, sometimes you eat the bear, and
sometimes, well, the bear eats you."*
"Is that some kind of Eastern thing?"[67]

KOAN

Chosui would sing the following refrain again and again:
   "Old Bear, are you in there?
   Old Bear, are you in there?"

REFLECTION

When the Old Bear came out of his cave in spring, he declared the
following: *My practice is to live in my own skin, not in the Buddha's
or my teacher's. When I was a cute cub a long time ago I thought I
was always wrong, so I had to confess and make things right before
I could get the good stuff, like honey and females. When I finally
began to do meditation, I started letting go of making things right.*

Is there anything as uncomfortable and painful as feeling basically *wrong*? There's the hollowness in the pit of the belly, or else so much prickly anxiety that your skin can barely contain all the self-criticism, self-reproach, and regrets. You feel like a bystander in your own life; others were given a starring role in theirs but you're merely a supporting actor in yours. You slouch, you can't meet others' eyes, or else you talk in a low voice as though you're not meant to be heard. You feel unnatural in your own body.

If someone's actions harm you, do you conclude there's something wrong with them? How about your partner, your child, a family member, or someone at work? When they do something positive in your eyes, is there now something right with them? What do *right* and *wrong* have to do with Buddha Nature?

In fact, what do right and wrong have to do with your nature, or anyone else's? How do you feel after you've done a good day of work and your boss congratulates you on a job well done? And how do you feel after being criticized, or even getting no reaction at all? Are there any less adequate measures of a human being than *right/wrong*? Life lies in experiencing the fullness of things, but instead, many of us listen to an internal critical voice that relentlessly hammers us down to size.

Is it any wonder that we avoid spending much time with ourselves? Instead of appreciating our life we cloud our senses with alcohol or drugs, watch our computers and televisions for hours, or else drown ourselves in activity.

Scratchy situations can be great teachers. If something itches, do you scratch back right away? When there's an irritation inside, do you invoke judgment or reaction?

When my husband had his major stroke, I'd see him lying in his hospital bed between therapies and looking at the opposite wall. "What are you thinking about?" I'd ask him.

"I'm not thinking," he'd say.

"Are you okay?"

In response, he'd make this motion with his one functioning arm that seemed to envelop the room, the busy hallways, the light, the dark, the hospital, and everything that lay beyond.

In the face of my alarm and need for reassurance, he was just quietly taking in his life, heartbeat after heartbeat. He was bearing witness to the question: *Old Bear, are you in there?*

I have watched bears in the forest and even in our backyard over the years, and can only admire how solid they are in the middle, how strong and stable even while standing on two hind legs to reach for a birdfeeder. They naturally live inside their own skin. This enables them to be incredibly versatile, run fast despite their weight, climb trees, swim across wide rivers, and derive nutrients from a wide variety of vegetation, nuts, berries, and fruit, not to mention insects and animals. They're solid and adaptable.

Isn't that what meditation gives us? Don't we learn to be solid in our belly, attuned to our breath? Don't we learn how to sit still, and when we rise go about our business, living our life fully and completely while performing a wide variety of tasks and playing many different roles?

The forty-second patriarch was Priest Liang-shan.
He studied with T'ung-an the Latter and served him.
T'ung-an asked him, "What is the business beneath the patch robe?"[68]

Whether it's a teacher's robe you're wearing, a business suit, a nurse's whites, a T-shirt, or just your own skin, aren't these all disguises? The question is the same: What lies beneath? Without thinking right or wrong, without thinking good or bad, what is it?

The answer T'ung-an gave was one word: *Intimacy.* But you must come up with your own answer.

We keep ourselves company for an entire lifetime. Our parents die, our children leave home, our friends and spouses go away or die. At first, pimples and freckles appear on our skin. Much later, we find pockmarks, wrinkles, varicose veins, and sunspots. Nevertheless, we continue to abide in our own skin, lined and wrinkled as it becomes. What does it take to feel comfortable in your skin?

An old Jewish prayer that we have included in our Zen Buddhist liturgy goes:

This is our life, the length of our days.
Day and night we meditate upon it.

———

Are there times when you feel invisible? Is this humility or is it hiding? Where does discomfort lie? What are you leaving out of intimacy?

Ando Feeds Her Hungry Spirit

Calling all the hungry hearts
Everywhere through endless time.
Your joy and your sorrow
I make it mine.[69]

KOAN

One day Ando received a notice of a rent increase. The notice triggered painful memories of her being abandoned on a New York street at age nine with a bag of clothes. Reading the notice, she was overcome by the hungry spirit of abandonment, with its wrenching emotional turmoil. After a few days, she went out to a nearby eatery for lunch. She saw a homeless man in line—dirty, smelly, and incoherent—scrounging in his pockets for money to pay for his food. Everyone was ignoring him, and the young cashier was doing her best to be kind. Spontaneously, Ando told the cashier, "I'll pay for his lunch." Ando suddenly felt a shift.

REFLECTION

How do you feed a hungry spirit? The hungry spirit is not some other person, but rather the insatiable part of yourself. In the ceremony of Feeding the Hungry Spirits as practiced by the Zen Peacemakers, inviting in the hungry spirit is a first step in changing your relationship to it. Although the hunger is already a part of you, you have likely expended a lot of energy keeping it at bay. Thus you must intentionally invite it in. This invitation is the beginning of changing your relationship to it.

Ando was so besieged by the hungry spirit of abandonment that her usual strategies of coping—meditating, staying present to her feelings and physical sensations, and talking to friends and family—did not bring her relief. What do you do when emotional pain paralyzes you? Do you instinctively reach for your favorite comfort food, drugs, or alcoholic beverage? When you feel enclosed in an emotional echo-chamber, do you become a couch-potato lost in mindless television shows or escape into shopping, sleep, or sex? How do you meet the turmoil of entangling thoughts and feelings?

As a longtime meditator, Ando instinctively bore witness to the sensations triggered within her body-mind by the rent increase notice. She recognized her habitual reflexes of clinging to the feelings and stories and also of wanting to push them away. She chose to remain face to face with her suffering. Whenever you choose to return to your breath in meditation, you strengthen the spiritual muscles needed for not clinging to or identifying with a particular storyline. You develop the capacity to be aware in the midst of even extreme discomfort. The very posture of meditation is one of stability and openness. Self-grasping, story-spinning, and difficult sensations continue to arise, but you are able to remain naked and open in the midst of it. Attention strengthens, awareness sharpens, and acceptance of what is takes root.

So it was for Ando. When it comes to childhood trauma, healing is a lifelong journey. You cannot control what will trigger painful emotional memories, but you can develop the skillful means to respond to them. After several stressful days of abiding naked and open in this desolate inner landscape, Ando went for lunch at the Burger Lounge. There she saw a homeless man—dirty and smelly, incoherent, scrounging in his pockets for money to pay for his meal—who reflected the inner terror of homelessness and abandonment that she had felt during the past days. Without hesitation, Ando said quietly to the cashier, "I'll pay for his lunch." Through this simple, spontaneous, and anonymous act, Ando felt inner peace returning for the first time in days and the sense of abandonment dissipated.

What shifted for Ando?

What opens for you when your own suffering meets the suffering of another person?

There is a line in the liturgy for feeding the hungry spirits: "Sharing your distress, I offer you this food, hoping to resolve your thirsts and hungers." The fire of the past days had forged in Ando a heart acutely receptive to the suffering of the homeless man and illuminated their shared distress and shared humanity. There were many people in the restaurant, but Ando alone responded without hesitation to the suffering right before her. In feeding the homeless man, Ando herself was fed. Your hunger and my hunger are not one, not two. Whatever you are feeling, someone else is feeling it, too.

So now, show me, how do you feed your hungry spirit?

What is the insatiable part of yourself? Can you invite it in? Paying for the homeless man's lunch was not a mere act of charity. Why not?

Nomita Sees the Ancestors

Before you were born.
Before your parents were born.
What do you call it?

KOAN

When Nomita was visiting her sister at the hospital, she passed a stranger in the hospital corridor and saw a long column of his ancestors walking behind him.

"Oh," she whispered to herself, "each of us is a combination of our ancestors." Throughout the day, whenever she looked at people, she saw their ancestors walking in an endless column behind them.

REFLECTION

Zen Master Guishan once told a student, "I, an old monk, will be reborn as a water buffalo in the front house of the temple a hundred years hence, and five words will be on the buffalo's side: *Monk Guishan, such and such*. If you call this water buffalo Monk

Guishan, it is still a water buffalo. If you call it a water buffalo, it is still Monk Guishan such and such. Tell me, what do you call it?"[70] Indeed, what do you call this life of complete connection?

When my sister, brother, and I are talking around the kitchen table, I am struck by how alike we are in our mannerisms and tone of voice. Our viewpoints, habits, and inclinations are unique to each of us, but there is an unmistakable commonality. I recall being amused when another sister of mine would complain about our mother because my sister's mannerisms—her tone of voice, rhythm of speech, and gestures—were exactly those of our mother. But could she see that?

The Zen tradition is steeped in stories about the Zen ancestors—each one is *my* ancestor, I was told. Each one took up a vow to wake up to the Great Matter of birth and death and to keep the awakened life alive. In Zen koan training, you learn to play freely with the ancestors by closing the gap between yourself and Master Guishan, for example. Right here, right now, the communal feast of ancestors is in full swing. They are all here, in your very body, chopping carrots, sweeping the floor, and tapping on computer keys.

The life of complete connection invites you to swallow the whole messy lot of ancestors in one gulp. For example, when the Southern white journalist Karen Branan delved into her ancestors, she discovered that within her biracial family a white ancestor had lynched a black ancestor.[71] So tell me, what have you actually inherited? When my dharma sister Jishu died, I asked myself, *What happens now to her vow to serve the children of the impoverished?* She had worked night and day to establish a childcare center that would include children of all races and income levels. Then I got it: You and I pick up the vow. You and I inherit the ancestor's passion, caring, and selfless capacity to serve others. We inherit the capacity to respond to our own lives with compassion, clarity, and intimacy. We inherit the potential to realize who we truly are.

When Nomita saw the long lines of ancestors, she realized that the ancestors are always right here. Today, through DNA testing, you can discover those with whom you share the same genes. When one of my students was diagnosed with breast cancer, she underwent genetic counseling. During her counseling session, she was guided through her family DNA tree, which included relatives that she had been estranged from for decades. "You know," she said, "there they all were in the room with me. I realized that you can disown people, but you cannot kick them out of the net." Genetic lineages are one thing, but tell me: Whom do you see that you do not recognize as yourself? Is it a family member that you no longer speak to? Is it the homeless woman living in the tent outside your house? The young child separated from his parents at the border? The gang member with tattoos across his forehead? And how about entire societies and cultures against which systemic discrimination is practiced? Tell me: What is the gap that needs to be closed?

———

When you look in the mirror, who do you see? Where are the ancestors right now? What are you leaving for others as your spiritual inheritance?

FOOTNOTES

1. *Entangling Vines: A Classic Collection of Zen Koans.* Translated and annotated by Thomas Yūhō Kirchner. Wisdom Publications, Somerville, MA, 2013, p. 134.

2. Maezumi, Taizan. *Appreciate Your Life: The Essence of Zen Practice.* Shambhala Publications, Boston, MA, 2001, p. 26.

3. *Moon in a Dewdrop: Writings of Zen Master Dogen.* Edited by Kazuaki Tanahashi. North Point Press, New York, NY, 1985, p. 75.

4. *The Diamond Sutra: The Perfection of Wisdom.* Translated with commentary by Red Pine. Counterpoint Press, Berkeley, CA, 2001, p. 27.

5. Kinnell, Galway. *Collected Poems.* The Literary Estate of Galway Kinnell. Houghton Mifflin Harcourt Publishing Co., New York, NY, 2017, p. 556.

6. John 12:45 *from Good News Bible.* American Bible Society, Philadelphia, PA, 1976, p. 145.

7. *The Gateless Gate: The Classic Book of Zen Koans.* Translated with commentary by Zen master Koun Yamada. The University of Arizona Press, Tucson, AZ, 2004, p. 153.

8. MacInnes, Elaine. *The Flowing Bridge: Guidance on Beginning Zen Koans.* Wisdom Publications, Somerville, MA, 2007, p. 53.

9. Rumi. *"Story II" from The Masnavi, Book IV.* Translated and abridged in *Masnaví-i Ma'naví, the Spiritual Couplets of Mauláná Jalálu'd-din Muhammad Balkhi* by Edward Henry Whinfield, 1898. Oxford University Press, UK, 2017.

10. *The Blue Cliff Record.* Translated by Thomas and J. C. Cleary. Shambhala Publications, Boston, MA, 1977, p. 172.

11. Zen Master Dogen. *Beyond Thinking: A Guide to Zen Meditation.* Edited by Kazuaki Tanahashi. Shambhala Publications, Boston, MA, 2004, p. 5.

12. Buddhism identifies our mind, dealing with mental objects, as our sixth sense.

13. "How to Answer a Knock on the Door." wikiHow, updated 18 November 2018, wikihow.com/Answer-a-Knock-on-the-Door, accessed 26 March 2019.

14. *The Gateless Gate: The Classic Book of Zen Koans.* Translated with commentary by Zen master Koun Yamada. The University of Arizona Press, Tucson, AZ, 1997, p. 53.

15. Merton, Thomas. *Conjectures of a Guilty Bystander.* The Abbey of Gethsemani. Doubleday Religion, New York, NY, 1966, p. 73.

16. Shibayama, Zenkei. *Zen Comments on the Mumonkan*: The Authoritative Translation, with Commentary, of a Basic Zen Text. Translated by Sumiko Kudo. Harper & Row, New York, NY, 1974, p. 209.

17. Lusseyran, Jacques. *And There Was Light: The Extraordinary Memoir of a Blind Hero of the French Resistance in World War II.* New World Library, Novato, CA, 2014.

18. Sheng Yen. *Subtle Wisdom: Understanding Suffering, Cultivating Compassion Through Ch'an Buddhism.* Dharma Drum Publications, Elmhurst, NY, 1999, pp. 74-5.

19. Rohr, Richard. *Everything Belongs: The Gift of Contemplative Prayer.* The Crossroad Publishing Company, New York, NY, 2003, p. 19.

20. Hemingway, Ernest. *A Farewell to Arms.* Charles Scribner's Sons, New York, NY, 1929, p. 249.

21. *The Blue Cliff Record.* Translated by Thomas and J. C. Cleary. Prajna Press, Boulder, CO, 1978, p. 395.

22. O'Donohue, John. *Conamara Blues.* HarperCollins Publishers, New York, NY, 2001, p. 23.

23. Shibayama, Zenkei. *Zen Comments on the Mumonkan: The Authoritative Translation*, with Commentary, of a Basic Zen Text. Translated by Sumiko Kudo. Harper & Row, New York, NY, 1974, p. 10.

24. Xiangyan Zhixian, as quoted by Eihei Dogen. *Treasury of the True Dharma Eye: Zen Master Dogen's Shobo Genzo.* Edited by Kazuaki Tanahashi. Shambhala Publications, Boston, MA, 2013, p. 444.

25. "David Grossman at the Joint Israeli-Palestinian Memorial Day Ceremony," JCall, 19 April 2018, https://en.jcall.eu/featured/david-grossman-at-the-joint-israeli-palestinian-memorial-day-ceremony, accessed April 2018.

26. *The Record of Transmitting the Light: Zen Master Keizan's Denkoroku.* Translated by Francis Dojun Cook. Wisdom Publications, Somerville, MA, 2003, p. 29.

27. *Shōbōgenzō-zuimonki: Sayings of Eihei Dogen Zenji, Recorded by Koun Ejō.* Translated by Shohaku Okumura. Soto-shu Shumucho, Tokyo, Japan, 2004, p. 140.

28. Chan Master Sheng Yen. *The Infinite Mirror: Commentaries on Two Chan Classics.* Shambhala Publications, Boston, MA, 1990, p. 35.

29. *Book of Serenity: One Hundred Zen Dialogues.* Translated by Thomas Cleary. Lindisfarne Press, Hudson, NY, 1990, p. 352.

30. Shibayama, Zenkei. *Zen Comments on the Mumonkan: The Authoritative Translation*, with Commentary, of a Basic Zen Text. Translated by Sumiko Kudo. Harper & Row, New York, NY, 1974, p. 99.

31. Carroll, Lewis. *Through the Looking-Glass, and What Alice Found There.* The Pennyroyal Press, London, England, 1983, p. 23.

32. Shibayama, Zenkei. *Zen Comments on the Mumonkan: The Authoritative Translation*, with Commentary, of a Basic Zen Text. Translated by Sumiko Kudo. Harper & Row, New York, NY, 1974, p. 140.

33. Heschel, Abraham Joshua. *The Sabbath: Its Meaning for Modern Man.* Farrar, Straus & Giroux, New York, NY, 2005, p. 220.

34. Dogen, Eihei. *Fukanzazengi.* Translated by Masao Abe and Norman Waddell. *The Eastern Buddhist, Vol. VI, No. 2,* 1973, p. 122.

35. One of the Lojong Slogan Cards entitled *"The Seven Points of Training the Mind."* 36. MacInnes, Elaine. *The Flowing Bridge: Guidance on Beginning Zen Koans.* Wisdom Publications, Somerville, MA, 2007, p. 33.

37. Boyle, Greg. "Father Greg Boyle: I Thought I Could 'Save' Gang Members. I Was Wrong." *America Magazine: The Jesuit Review*, 28 March 2017.

38. Dogen, Eihei, *"Genjo Koan."* Translated by Robert Aitken and Kazuaki Tanahashi in *The Way of Everyday Life: Zen Master Dogen's Genjokoan*, and revised by Taizan Maezumi and Francis Dojun Cook. Center Publications, Los Angeles, CA, 1978.

39. Dogen Zenji, Eihei. *Dōgen's Genjo Koan: Three Commentaries.* Counterpoint, Berkeley, CA, 2011, p. 223.

40. Connelly, Ben. *Inside Vasubandhu's Yogacara: A Practitioner's Guide.* Wisdom Publications, Somerville, MA, 2016, p. 197.

41. *"Samyutta Nikaya,"* as it appears in Wes Nisker's *Buddha's Nature: A Practical Guide to Discovering Your Place in the Cosmos.* Bantam, New York, NY, 2000, p. 33.

42. *"Heart Sutra,"* as it appears in Bernie Glassman's *Infinite Circle: Teachings in Zen.* Shambhala Publications, Boston, MA, 2002, p. 3.

43. Eliot, T. S. *Four Quartets.* Gardners Books, Eastbourne, UK, 2001, p. 43.

44. *Dōgen's Extensive Record: A Translation of the Eihei Kōroku.* Translated by Taigen Dan Leighton and Shohaku Okumura. Wisdom Publications, Somerville, MA, 2004, p. 349.

45. *The Lotus Sutra.* Translated by Burton Watson. Columbia University Press, New York, NY, 1993, p. 229.

46. Maezumi, Taizan. *Appreciate your Life: The Essence of Zen Practice,* Shambhala Publications, Boston, MA, 2001, p. 114.

47. Sokuo, Eto. *Zen Master Dogen as Founding Patriarch.* Translated by Shohei Ichimura. North American Institute of Zen and Buddhist Studies, Tokyo, Japan, 2001, p. 551.

48. Cacciatore, Joanne. *Bearing the Unbearable: Love, Loss, and the Heartbreaking Path of Grief.* Wisdom Publications, Somerville, MA, 2017, p. 174.

49. *The Blue Cliff Record.* Translated by Thomas and J.C. Cleary. Shambhala Publications, Boston, MA, 1992, p. 249.

50. *The Blue Cliff Record.* Translated by Thomas and J. C. Cleary. Prajna Press, Boulder, CO, 1978, p. 365.

51. Ikkyū Sōjun death poem, appearing in John Stevens' *Three Zen Masters: Ikkyū, Hakuin, Ryōkan.* Kodansha International, New York, NY, 1993, p. 56.

52. The closing chant sung every evening in the Zen meditation hall.

53. Zen Peacemaker Order Precept: *Not Elevating Oneself and Blaming Others.*

54. Boyle, Greg. *Barking to the Choir: The Power of Radical Kinship.* Simon & Schuster, New York, NY, 2017, p. 132.

55. *"To You": Collection of Sayings by Kodo Sawaki.* Compiled by Uchiyama Kosho. Translated by Muho Noelke and Reiho Haasch. Published on the Antai-ji Temple of Peace website: antaiji.org.

56. *The Blue Cliff Record.* Translated by Thomas and J. C. Cleary. Shambhala Publications, Boston, MA, 1977, p. 72.

57. *Zen Flesh, Zen Bones: A Collection of Zen and Pre-Zen Writings.* Compiled by Paul Reps. Doubleday & Company, Garden City, NY, p. 5.

58. Maezumi, Taizan. *Appreciate Your Life: The Essence of Zen Practice.* Shambhala Publications, Boston, MA, 2001, p. xi.

59. Dogen, Eihei. *Fukanzazengi.* Translated by Norman Waddell and Masao Abe. *The Eastern Buddhist, Vol I, No. 2,* 1973, p. 121.

60. Beck, Charlotte Joko. *Nothing Special: Living Zen.* HarperCollins, San Francisco, CA, 1994, p. 168.

61. Wick, Gerry Shishin. *The Book of Equanimity: Illuminating Classic Zen Koans*. Wisdom Publications, Somerville, MA, 2005, p. 63.

62. *The Gateless Gate: The Classic Book of Zen Koans*. Translated with commentary by Zen master Koun Yamada. The University of Arizona Press, Tucson, AZ, 1979. p. 31.

63. Mumon Roshi, Yamada. *Lectures on the Ten Oxherding Pictures*. Translated by Victor Sogen Hori. University of Hawaii Press, Honolulu, HI, 2004, p. 18.

64. Chan Master Hui Hai. *Zen Teaching of Instantaneous Awakening*. Translated by John Blofeld. Buddhist Publishing Group, London, United Kingdom, 1992, p. 107.

65. *The Blue Cliff Record*. Translated by Thomas and J. C. Cleary. Prajna Press, Boulder, CO, 1978, p. 583.

66. Berry, Wendell. *Openings: Poems*. Harcourt, New York, NY, 1980.

67. Coen, Ethan and Joel. *The Big Lebowski.*: Gramercy Pictures, United States, 1998.

68. *The Record of Transmitting the Light: Zen Master Keizan's Denkoroku*. Translated by Francis Dojun Cook. Center Publications, Los Angeles, CA, 1991, p. 190.

69. Krishna Das. *Chants of a Lifetime: Searching for a Heart of Gold*. Hay House, Inc., Carlsbad, CA, 2010, p. 186.

70. *Entangling Vines: A Classic Collection of Zen Koans*. Translated and annotated by Thomas Yūhō Kirchner. Wisdom Publications, Somerville, MA, 2013, p. 73.

71. Eligon, John. "Their Ancestors Were on Opposite Sides of a Lynching. Now, They're Friends." *The New York Times*, May 4, 2018.

ACKNOWLEDGMENTS

We are very grateful for the enthusiastic support and help that so many people gave towards the compilation of this book of householder koans.

Zen practitioners from around the world submitted koans from the edges of their lives, places that pained, provoked, and challenged, but also contained moments of sudden understanding, clarity, and joy. All of them have recognized the opportunity to practice in the crowded, busy landscape of a householder life.

Much appreciation to everyone who reviewed these koans and gave invaluable comments: Eberhard E. Fetz, Kipp Ryodo Hawley, Ilia Shinko Perez, Rose Pinard, Suzanne Shunryo Webber, and Gerry Shishin Wick. To the Priest Circle of the Zen Center of Los Angeles, and especially to Betsy Enduring-Vow Brown, Darla Myoho Fjeld, and Thomas Dharma-Joy Reichert. Many thanks, too, to Gemma Sōji Cubero del Barrio.

Our personal thanks to the sanghas of the Green River Zen Center and the Zen Center of Los Angeles for their support of this project, and for providing the energy field where all our delusions, turned time and time again, beneath sun and rain, become fertile ground for awakening.

Eve Myonen Marko   *Wendy Egyoku Nakao*
Massachusetts   *California*
2018   *2018*

ABOUT THE AUTHORS

Roshi Eve Myonen Marko is the resident teacher at the Green River Zen Center in Massachusetts and a Founding Teacher of the Zen Peacemaker Order. She co-founded Peacemaker Circle International with her husband, Bernie Glassman, linking and training spiritually-based peacemakers in the US, Europe, and the Middle East. She served as Spiritholder at Zen Peacemakers' bearing witness retreats at Auschwitz-Birkenau, Rwanda, and the Black Hills with Lakota elders. She blogs at www.evemarko.com.

Roshi Wendy Egyoku Nakao is the Abbot Emeritus (1999-2019) of the Zen Center of Los Angeles (ZCLA), having succeeded the late Roshi Bernie Glassman as the third Abbot in 1999. She currently serves as ZCLA's head teacher and head priest. She ordained as a Zen priest in 1983 and trained with her root teacher, Venerable Taizan Maezumi, at ZCLA until his death in 1995. She became a Dharma Successor of Roshi Bernie Glassman in 1996 in Yonkers, NY, and is a founding teacher of the Zen Peacemaker Order, which promotes spiritually-based social activism.

Printed in the USA
CPSIA information can be obtained
at www.ICGtesting.com
JSHW021333130824
68065JS00002B/123